JUST ... THINK ABOUT IT

Peg Tittle

Magenta

Just ... Think about It
Copyright 2018 by Peg Tittle

Magenta

ISBN 978-1-926891-34-7 epub
ISBN 978-1-926891-35-4 mobi
ISBN 978-1-926891-38-5 pdf
ISBN 978-1-926891-57-6 print

cover design by: Peg Tittle and Elizabeth Beeton

pegtittle.com

All rights reserved. Without limiting the rights under copyright reserved above, no part of this publication may be reproduced, stored in or introduced into a retrieval system, or transmitted, in any form, or by any means (electronic, mechanical, photocopying, recording, or otherwise) without the prior written permission of both the copyright owner and the above publisher of this book.

Acknowledgements

Earlier versions of the following pieces have appeared on *The Philosophy Magazine's* online Philosophy Cafe: "Useless Humanities," "Speaking in Code," "I Don't Have a Conscience," "Garbage," "Sex, like Religion/Religion, like Sex," "Airbands and Power Point," "To Connect," "Appropriation or Imagination?", "Unprofessional," "The Absence of Imagination," "Religion, Superstition, and Habit," "Visionary," and "'I killed you. Killed you too. Got you.' In the Library."

Earlier versions of the following pieces have appeared at the *Institute for Ethics and Emerging Technologies* website: "Why Teaching Business Ethics can be Difficult", "Business Rules the World. Do We Want It To?", "Ethics without Philosophers," "Making Certain Words Illegal," and "Assisted Suicide and Unassisted Suicide: What's the Difference?"

Earlier versions of the following pieces were published in *Humanist in Canada*: "New and Improved/Needs and Wants" (reprinted in *South Australian Humanist*), "Appropriation or Imagination," "Cultural Anarchy," and "Assisted Suicide and Unassisted Suicide: What's the Difference?"

Earlier versions of the following pieces were published in *Academic Exchange Quarterly*: "Digital Thought," "The Absence of Imagination," and "In Praise of Dead Air" (the last-mentioned also appeared in *Philosophy Now*).

Earlier versions of "Every Day in Every Way" and "To Connect" were published in *Links*.

"To Connect" was also published in *Elenchus*, along with "Congratulations."

"Stop Being Complicit" and "Responding to Wolf Whistles" have appeared on the BlogHer website.

"Air Bands and Power Point" was published in *Forum* and *Indirections*.

An earlier version of "Our Christian Language" was published in *Free Inquiry*.

Also by Peg Tittle

It Wasn't Enough (Inanna, 2020)
Exile (Rock's Mills Press, 2018)
What Happened to Tom (Inanna, 2016)

Sexist Shit that Pisses Me Off (Magenta, 2014)
No End to the Shit that Pisses Me Off (Magenta, 2013)
Still More Shit that Pisses Me Off (Magenta, 2012)
More Shit that Pisses Me Off (Magenta, 2012)
Shit that Pisses Me Off (Magenta, 2011)

Ethical Issues in Business:Inquiries, Cases, and Readings 2e (Broadview, 2016)
Critical Thinking: An Appeal to Reason (Routledge, 2011)
What If ... Collected Thought Experiments in Philosophy (Pearson, 2004)
Should Parents be Licensed? Debating the Issues (Prometheus, 2004)

CONTENTS

Preface
1. Garbage
2. Who owns the water?
3. New and Improved / Needs and Wants
4. Canada Day – Are you sure you want to celebrate?
5. Life as we know it
6. Have you noticed the way the weather is being reported?
7. Business in Denial
8. No Advertising in Public Space
9. No Advertising
10. Supervisory Responsibility
11. Leadership?
12. Crossing the Line
13. Mentoring: It's who you know
14. Unprofessional
15. Ethics without Philosophers
16. Why Teaching Business Ethics can be Difficult
17. Business Rules the World. Do we want it to?
18. Change the way we do business
19. To Connect
20. The Absence of Imagination
21. Air Bands and Power Point
22. What do you want me to say?
23. Sexism and Teaching: The Elephant in the Room
24. Visionary
25. Useless Humanities
26. Dismissing Philosophy and Philosophers / Philosophy – Misunderstood
27. How Many Specialists does it take to Change a Lightbulb?
28. Religion: Superstition and Habit (a very brief primer)
29. Sex, like Religion / Religion, like Sex
30. I Don't Have a Conscience
31. Our Christian Language

32. Acts of God
33. Appropriation or Imagination?
34. Cultural Anarchy
35. Government Grants to Natives for Grad School
36. Taxing the Rich
37. Private Property and Visual Intrusion
38. Noise Trespass
39. On Power Outages
40. An Open Letter to Weekenders Everywhere
41. Making Certain Words Illegal
42. "I killed you. Killed you too. Got you." In the Library.
43. What's wrong with selling your organs?
44. Assisted Suicide and Unassisted Suicide: What's the Difference?
45. Rising above Natural Selection
46. The Inconsistency of Not Requiring Parents to be Licensed
47. Legislating Prenatal Care
48. Telling our Members of Parliament What to Wear
49. The Problem with Democracy
50. Snowmobiles Rule – Only in Canada. Pity.
51. Rich Rednecks
52. How to Make a Man Grow Up
53. Rules of Combat
54. Responding to Wolf-Whistles
55. Just tell me what to say and I'll say it
56. *The Last Man on Earth* Explains Everything
57. *13 Reasons Why*
58. Slutwalk: What's the Problem?
59. Stop Being Complicit in your own Subordination
60. This is your brain. This is your brain on oxytocin: Mom.
61. Ugly, Fat, Hairy Feminists
62. The Trouble with Trans
63. The "M" Word on Prime Time TV!!
64. Artificial Intelligence Indeed
65. The Adult Market
66. Women Discover Life on Mars

67. We Won!
68. Congratulations!
69. Getting Married
70. Reading/Watching the News: A Bad Habit
71. Vote? WTF?
72. Speaking in Code
73. If you can't say anything nice, don't say anything at all.
74. In Praise of Dead Air
75. YouTube: 300 hours per minute
76. Digital Thought
77. Asking the Right Questions
78. Good Intentions: The Road to Hell (and justifiably so)
79. Planning is Sinister?
80. Every Day in Every Way
81. "If my wife will let me."
82. Men Need to Reclaim the Moral
83. Oh the horror.
84. Calm down. Don't think about – Don't think.

Preface

In a way, *Just ... Think about It* is part of my *Shit that Pisses Me Off* series, but it seemed to me that too many people were misled by the title and the covers of the series, dismissing the pieces as emotional rants, failing to see that in very many cases, I was actually presenting arguments worth serious consideration.

So ... new title and new cover.

When there are several pieces dealing with the same broad topic (for example, our environment, business, education, religion, legislation, etc.), I've put them together in a cluster (rather than a separate titled section, which seemed too monumental).

Garbage

I was walking down the lane the other day and I noticed a piece of litter, looked like the melted bottom of a plastic bottle. I fumed for a bit, angry at whoever had just tossed it there, and planned to pick it up on my way back. To carry it all the way home, where I'd throw it in the garbage, and three weeks later take to the dump. And it suddenly occurred to me: why go to all that trouble just so it could be buried in some arbitrary place six miles away from here, when I could just as easily bury it here?

But it's not so arbitrary, is it. It's '*away* from here', it's not on the lane I walk on every day, it's not in my backyard. And I realized then that when city planners started including dumps in their blueprints, we took a seriously wrong turn: with such a word, such a concept, we legitimized NIMBY. So too with words like 'litter' and 'garbage'. What is that but stuff that doesn't belong here, stuff we *don't want here*, here in *our* back yard. We 'throw it away'.

And where is 'away'? It's a piece of land bought or rented for just that purpose; a bunch of people, the city, the community, has simply pooled their money, their taxes, to hire someone to pick up and move the stuff we don't want, from 'here' to 'there'. ('There' being, often, not even in our own country.) (Explain again how the rich nations came to be so rich?)

Now that might not be so bad, but let's go back to square one: why? *Why did the people want the stuff moved in the first place?* Because it's unhealthy and/or unsightly. The stockholder model (I own, therefore I have the right to ...) is simplistic, in denial with regard to relationships, to interdependence. The stakeholder model (I am affected by, therefore I have the right to ...) is more enlightened. And since the stuff we put in the dump, the 'landfill' site (ya gotta love euphemisms), can degrade the land, water, and air *beyond* its borders, no, we don't have the right, even though we have the money, to pay someone to move it from our back yard to someone else's back yard. (Actually, it can affect other people even if it *stays* in our backyard. Because it doesn't really. Stay there. So we don't even have the right to dump it, even to *produce* it – if it's going to end up dumped, in the first place.)

Imagine a world in which there was no word for 'garbage'. Perhaps if there was no such thing as 'the dump', if we didn't have a 'waste' basket in every room, perhaps then we wouldn't buy so many plastic bottles. There's only so many you can bury. They don't decompose. Perhaps instead, we'd buy our cola as concentrate in bottles half the size or as fizz tablets wrapped in paper. Perhaps we'd buy only reusables, only compostables. My god if we'd had to keep on our own half-acre or in our own apartment everything we've ever thrown out ...

Who owns the water?

I am intrigued by (occasional) struggles over ownership of water – not so much the issue of whether or not Canada should sell its lakes, but whether or not they are Canada's to sell. And what intrigues me is not that we're struggling with ownership of water, but that we're *not* struggling with ownership of land. We accept that concept: someone owns the land and when you want some, you have to buy it from the owner, who bought it from the previous owner, and so on. Why isn't the same true for our water?

Is this inconsistency due to our being 'solids' as *Star Trek Voyager's* Odo might note? (Solids who, nevertheless, need liquids, as well as gases – and we haven't even *begun* to consider ownership of the air – to survive.) (And, further, who are *themselves* mostly liquid and partly gas ...) Or is it an indication of our bias toward the visual – we can't see air nor can we draw lines in water. Whatever, it is certainly not the result of rational consideration.

New and Improved / Needs and Wants

'New and improved' is not just a bit of harmless puffery; it's a two-party addiction. Stupid consumers must have and stupid companies must produce – new and improved stuff. And it hurts third parties. Such as the animals who are used to test a product every time it changes, every time it becomes new and improved. And, perhaps more importantly (though I'm really not sure anymore), the people who won't get their needs met because resources are being spent on stupid people's wants.

There is a difference. Between needs and wants. One you can do without; the other you can't. People like to call wants 'needs', however, because needs are more *compelling*. Such people are thus being manipulative: to say 'I need X' makes it sound like it's not an option, like X must be provided; but to say 'I want X' leaves the other free(r) not to fulfil the request. We need clean water, nutritious food, shelter/warmth, and sometimes, medical care. Everything else is a want. (So yes, Freud and Maslow and every man since who says sex is a need – you're wrong. Evidence supports the contrary claim: surprising as this may seem, people who don't have sex do not die.)

Nor do you die without the new and improved dish detergent or lip gloss. Or this year's Chrysler. Don't get me wrong: many improvements are indeed improvements; some are even valuable improvements. The new detergents with*out* phosphates are much better than the ones with phosphates. And the car with the catalytic converter and higher mpg is better than its predecessor. But most changes are not improvements. (There is a difference – between change and improvement.) And most improvements are not significant enough to warrant new and improved products at the rate they're being put on the market.

Most of the new and improved stuff is stuff we don't need.

Actually, so is most of the old and unimproved stuff. There's a frighteningly high number of people in our society who exhibit arrested development, who seem stuck at the infantile phase of shouting 'More! More! I want more!' I yearn for the day when kids across our country do not start each day reciting a prayer or an anthem but the words 'We don't need.' Because, by and large, in Canada, we don't. We don't need. We already have. Enough.

Growth is not always good. We have these positive associations with the word because we think of a child growing. But the healthy child stops growing when it reaches an optimum size. There's a name for unlimited growth: cancer.

And it's this not stopping, it's this making and taking more than we need, that has gotten us into this dead end. Our atmospheric carbon dioxide, largely the consequence of our resource consumption, is [in February 2018] at 408.5ppm (which, barring an immediate and international response, assures a global temperature increase of 2 degrees. Which triggers a bunch of feedback loops we can't stop) [1]. Isn't it time to stop? To grow up and say 'No thank you, I'm fine, I have enough'?

---

1. See https://www.scientificamerican.com/article/earth-will-cross-the-climate-danger-threshold-by-2036/ and https://www.cbsnews.com/news/paris-un-climate-talks-why-2-degrees-are-so-important/.

Canada Day – Are you sure you want to celebrate?

Before you get all patriotic and fly your little Canadian flags in celebration of Canada Day and, presumably, of being Canadian, think about it. Are you really proud to be:
- the second worst of all the industrialized countries when it comes to sulfur dioxide emissions
- the second worst when it comes to carbon monoxide emissions
- the third worst when it comes to greenhouse gas emissions (we pump out 48% more greenhouse gas emissions per capita than the OECD average, up about 13% since 1990, in violation of our international commitments)
- the fourth worst when it comes to producing ozone-depleting stuff
- the second worst with regard to per capita water consumption
- the third worst when it comes to per capita energy consumption
- the second worst when it comes to energy efficiency
- not even in the top ten with regard to garbage production per person (we're 18th out of 27) (and we're 24th out of 25 for glass recycling, 21st out of 28 for paper and cardboard recycling)
- when it comes to producing nuclear waste, we're #1!! Yay!! We produce more nuclear waste per person than any other OECD country!!

In short, we are hogs. We are stupid, don't-give-a-damn pigs. We're the ones to blame for so much of this climate change – the heat waves, the floods, the droughts, the high food prices. Our fault. Yup, fly your little flag. That's it, wave it, smile … Ya stupid idiot.

Canada vs. The OECD: An Environmental Comparison, David R. Boyd. Eco-Research Chair of Environmental Law and Policy, University of Victoria. 2001.
http://bibvir2.uqac.ca/archivage/12536745.pdf

Life as we know it

So I noticed this morning the birds are gone. They used to wake me up every morning around five o'clock and since I'd just gone to bed at two or three, I'd roll over, put in my earplugs, and go back to sleep. And I just realized that I haven't had to do this for … must be a week now.

And it occurred to me. This is how it will happen. This is how it *is* happening. I've been hoping for, waiting for, some catastrophic event, some wake-the-fuck-up change that will make the world sit up and take notice and finally, *finally*, do something to fix, to save, the planet.

But that's not going to happen.

When's the last time you saw a frog? A bee? Fish swimming in the water?

In March [2012], it's 80 degrees in Canada and 30 degrees in Greece, food prices have increased 25% because of droughts, and *still* people drive their cars into town several times a week, *still* people go on vacation by plane, and what's on TV? Nonstop coverage of the Olympics. Of people trying to run a little bit faster than someone else or throw a ball a little bit further than someone else.

So I'm pissed off again at everyone.

And I'm pissed off at the scientists. The point of no return has been moved from 2040 to 2017 [1]. It'll take just 2 degrees. We're at 1.6 degrees. [2] And what have they done? Quietly, politely, filed their reports. Continued to publish their papers in journals that only a dozen other people read. They should be taking political leaders hostage! They should be – I don't know, isn't there any way they can *force* someone to do something? Students organize protests against higher tuition, larger groups made the Occupy Wall Street movement happen – where are the scientists storming Ottawa and Washington saying "LOOK, YOU MOTHER FUCKERS, YOU HAVE TO DO SOMETHING NOW!!"?

And why isn't the rest of the world boycotting us? Telling us they won't buy any of our shit until we get our act together about the environment?

So, this is how it'll happen. First the frogs, then the bees, then the fish, then the birds ... Life as we know it will end while everyone in the States and Canada is watching TV. [3] Probably some new reality show.

---

1. "[As] the IEA found, we're about five years away from building enough carbon-spewing infrastructure to lock us in and make it extremely difficult – maybe impossible – to avoid 450 ppm. The point of no return comes around 2017."
http://www.washingtonpost.com/blogs/wonkblog/post/when-do-we-hit-the-point-of-no-return-for-climate-change/2011/11/10/gIQA4rri8M_blog.html
2. "In the last century, the average global temperature has risen approximately 1.6 degrees Fahrenheit; disconcertingly, most scientists agree that the point of no return is a rise 2 degrees Fahrenheit. Beyond these levels (approximated to be 450 ppm carbon dioxide), the planet will experience unprecedented changes in the global climate and a significant increase in the severity of natural disasters (Dresner, 2008). [...] [S]ome estimate that the loss of species is currently happening at 1000 times the natural rate of extinction (Esterman, 2010). Species simply do not have enough time to adapt to altered habitats or migrate to better suited ecosystems. This leaves them stranded, and many of them soon become endangered. ... [And in case you miss the relevance of that] As a population, humans depend on a great deal of species for survival."
http://web.mit.edu/12.000/www/m2015/2015/climatechange.html
3. An aside ... sort of ... I caught a glimpse, by accident, of one of those entertainment celebrity shows the other day and it hit me: we pay people who *pretend* to be doctors more than we pay people who actually *are* doctors.

Have you noticed the way the weather is being reported?

Have you noticed the way the weather is being reported lately?

Commentators refer to "extreme storms" – making them sound all exciting and daring, like "extreme sports".

One opens with "this week's wildest weather" as if we're on a fun safari.

Another asks "Will any records be broken?" suggesting that, like athletic competitions, breaking a record will be a good thing.

And on a popular weather network website, the "photo of the day" shows a huge iceberg afloat, testament to the alarming melt of the polar ice [1], and the caption reads, unbelievably, "Anyone else see a face in the iceberg?"

They've turned the death of our planet into entertainment.

And then there's all that pseudo-scientific detail! The rain is going to be caused by water droplets, that's droplets of H2O, in the air that will succumb to gravity, under normal conditions, and eventually reach us, possibly at 6:20 or maybe 6:21.

Thing is, all that drama and detail distracts us from what's really going on with the weather. Notice the obsession with proximate causes? Is it because if they addressed the real causes, those remote causes like eating meat and using fossil fuels, they'd have to address blame? (Maybe that's why they're referring to "acts of weather". Not, like, acts of humanity.) (And certainly not, anymore, acts of someone's god.)

And, have you noticed the increase in climate change disaster movies? Right, yeah, let's get everyone comfortable with the idea. The idea that survival is possible. All we need is a hero.

---

1. "Six thousand years ago, when the world was one degree warmer than it is now, the American agricultural heartland around Nebraska was desert. ... The effect of one-degree warming, therefore, requires no great feat of imagination. ... *Whilst snow-covered ice reflects more than 80% of the sun's heat, the darker ocean absorbs up to 95% of solar radiation. Once sea ice begins to melt, in other words, the process becomes self-reinforcing. More ocean surface is revealed, absorbing solar heat, raising temperatures and making it unlikelier that ice will re-form next winter. The disappearance of 720,000 square kilometres of supposedly permanent ice in a single year testifies to the rapidity of planetary change. ... Chance of avoiding one degree of global warming: zero.* http://globalwarming.berrens.nl/globalwarming.htm

Business in Denial

'We're just providing what the market, what people, demand.' The CEO says. 'The customer is squarely in the driver's seat.' Yeah right. Gosh, shucks, don't-look-at-me.

One, I doubt that's true. I mean, if people really wanted your product, you wouldn't (have to) spend millions on advertising, advertising to persuade them to buy it. Supply isn't (just) following demand; demand is following supply. *Your* supply. *You're* in the driver's seat.

Two, even if it is true, that people do want it, I find it hard to believe that someone with enough whatever to get to an executive position, a decision-making position, would be so meekly obedient to the desires, the demands, of the common people.

Or so helpless: 'demands' is such loaded language, implying that resistance, your resistance, is futile, implying that you are without power here.

Or so spineless – as if you have no mind, no desire, no will of your own.

Please, have the guts, the maturity, to take responsibility for your actions. You produce/provide what you do because you choose to, because you want to. If you *are* acceding to market demands – and I have no doubt that you are – it's because it's profitable, it's because (you think) it's in your best interests. You 'want to make it easy for the customer to do business with [you]' because business *with* you is business *for* you. Customers are a means to your end of profit. Otherwise you'd be as interested in poverty management as you are in wealth management.

'Our shareholders demand high returns.' Another pass-the-buck denial of responsibility. One, again, I doubt that's strictly true. Did you ask them all? And was their response fully informed? Were they aware that their high returns come at the expense of others? (Others' low wages, loss of employment; other's high prices, loss of choice through monopoly; environmental degradation; etc.)

And two, even if they do, again, do you have to obey them? Of course not. Unless – and here's the all important hidden (by you, from you) assumption – unless you want the value of your company to be 'high' so people will give you money. There's that self-interest again.

'Return on equity is an important measure of our success.' Not the amount of good one does, not the amount of happiness one creates, no, these things don't matter; success isn't even justice, isn't getting back what one puts out, no, success is how much *more* one gets back than one puts out. Self-interest. Literally, *interest. For the self.* It's egoism, pure and simple. And childish and dangerous. I don't think 'society as a whole' is in the vocabulary. The total inability to recognize, let alone deal with, the moral dimension – i.e., the consideration of *others* – is frightening.

And the ego knows no satisfaction. 'From start-up to growth.' The life cycle of a business seems to stop there. At growth. And more growth. And more growth. Excuse me? What about stasis? What about decline? They are part of the entire life cycle. Only a cancer grows and grows and grows.

No Advertising in Public Space

I once read a sci fi novel in which holographic ads suddenly appeared in front of you, 'blocking' your way, almost continuously, as you made your way down a city street. It made me imagine people paid by perfume companies wandering through the streets assailing me with sample sprays …

I am a strong advocate of prohibiting all advertising in public spaces. There is no justification for the desires of one person, let alone the desire of one person *for money*, to be imposed on everyone. Furthermore, there are enough alternative venues for advertising (radio, TV, newspapers, magazines, websites, malls), all of which, unlike, often, public space, can be used or not (especially as long as there are advertising-free radio, TV, magazine, and website options), making the use of public space is simply unnecessary.

We should be able to go about our lives without the constant assault on the senses, on the mind, that is advertising. Of course this is an argument made by someone who *notices* ads, who *pays attention* to her environment, who *thinks about* what she sees. For most people, ads are not such an assault, because they're unconsciously perceived. But then they're even more coercive, subliminally manipulative, and even more indefensible in public space.

Advertising is not only cognitively coercive, but physically dangerous when it appears on roadsides, especially in animated form, which shamelessly tries to take drivers' attention off the road. Would we allow drivers to watch TV, similarly visual content with moving images, while they drive?

An additional argument applies to natural environment public space (forest, field, lake, ocean) which is, to my mind, beautiful (or at least more beautiful than city). In this case, there is the added transgression of the destruction of beauty. It was a sad, sad day when advertising was allowed along the perimeter of the rink and even on the ice during figure skating performances. Years to achieve the perfect lines, sullied by persisting in-your-face BUY-MY-SHIT signs we can't help but see while we try to focus on the beauty. (And it's not like the sign enhances the beauty. It's not like the sign itself is remotely beautiful.)

    Would those of us who can hear allow a deaf person to make a clamour with cymbals all day long? Then why do we allow aesthetically-challenged CEOs to do the same? Why do we allow our natural beauty to be degraded, destroyed, piece by piece, by those who are, obviously, blind to its beauty? Is it because we don't recognize the beauty or because we don't value it (or, at least, don't value it over the individual pursuit of money). (Seriously? Do we really believe that an individual's desire for money trumps so much?) (Well, no, the people with the power to make regulations believe that. And they are as aesthetically-challenged. And often CEOs.)

No Advertising

Imagine a "No Advertising' rule. Whenever you wanted to buy something, you'd just look it up in a central directory with a really good search engine that enabled you to see all of your options (a shortlist based on your preferences) accompanied by product information. Or you could just choose from the selection offered by whatever store you went to.

Most magazines, newspapers, radio stations, and television stations would die. The ones that are just tools of the companies who use them for advertising. The other ones, the ones supported by people genuinely interested in reading, listening, and watching what they have to offer, would live on.

So that means that all those incredibly annoying DJs who sound hyper-enthusiastic about, well, everything – gone. All those TV stations full of all those inane TV shows that no one in their right mind would pay to see – gone. (And oh to watch a show without the station logo on the screen in my face the whole time. Has anyone actually proven that that increases how much I watch NBC or CBC or whoever? It's like the company name that was etched on the glass door of my woodstove; since I like to watch a fire without someone's name etched on my consciousness every time I do, I had the glass replaced. At an additional cost, of course.)

No more blinking billboards to distract us from driving. (Those things should be illegal in any case.)

No more flyers. All that time, labour, and material used by the company, the post office, and the recipient to deal with all that advertising – recovered, for other purposes.

No more telemarketing phone calls. (There's a reason there are no more door-to-door salesmen. We'd've shot 'em all by now.)

And my god, the internet. All those pages that would load twice as quickly if they didn't have ads.

Not to mention the email spam. Gone.

In all, over $500 billion would become available for other purposes. Instead of spending all that money to make their products *look* good, companies might use it to make products that actually *are* good. Did you know that the pharmaceutical industry spends twice as much on advertising as it does on research?

Lastly, freed from the constant onslaught of others telling us what we need and want, maybe we could recognize our genuine needs and wants.

Supervisory Responsibility

I have come to realize that the corporate definition of 'responsibility' is very different than the common definition. I am thinking, in particular, of 'supervisory responsibility'.

Consider this situation. A subordinate (say, an assistant) prepares and distributes advertisements for a position; she interviews various applicants, selects one and notifies him of his success, then trains the new person, and periodically checks his work performance. One might think the subordinate's job description would include "recruit, hire, train, and supervise".

One would be wrong. Subordinates can't hire. Only superordinates (supervisors) can hire. Subordinates can't supervise. Only superordinates can supervise. Say what? But the subordinate *did* hire and supervise, so obviously she *can* hire and supervise. Nope.

And apparently this set-up is common: the subordinate actually *does* X, but the superordinate is *responsible for* X. If there's a problem, he's the one who'll be held accountable.

First, there's a substantial incoherence here. If indeed the subordinate is *not* responsible, why is she reprimanded and sometimes even fired for making a mistake or doing a poor job? The notion of penalty implies the notion of responsibility. Why blame A for X if A isn't responsible? Shouldn't we blame whoever's responsible? Shouldn't the superordinate, then, be fired if the subordinate messes up? (Yeah right. That'll happen. When pigs fly.)

Second, this conception of responsibility infantilizes the subordinate. A sign of maturity is that one takes responsibility for one's actions. Only with children (and the mentally incompetent) is another held responsible. Denying the subordinate that responsibility is, then, insisting on juvenile (or incompetent) status.

Third, it puts a great deal of strain on the superordinate. It is very stressful to be responsible for someone else's behaviour. One has the responsibility, but not the control. No wonder they develop ulcers.

And no wonder they develop into control freaks – a fourth problem. If one is responsible for something, one is surely going to try to *have* some control over that something. And so superordinates try to control their subordinates: they give orders, they criticize, they reprimand, etc. The greater the subordinate's autonomy (insistence on maturity), the more antagonistic the relationship will become.

Fifth, there's an ethical problem. It's simply not fair to hold people responsible for something over which they have no control. This moral principle is even threaded throughout our legal system.

This conception of responsibility is unfair in another way as well, and this is a sixth problem. Usually, one of the relevant aspects of a job description that determines the salary for that position is degree of responsibility. So the subordinate does X, and is awarded, say, 10 points on the salary scale. But the superordinate is *responsible for* X, and is awarded 100 points. Not fair.

This logical sleight-of-hand makes the superordinate's job look so much more demanding – after all, they're responsible for so very much: if they supervise ten people, they're responsible for ten whole jobs! No wonder they get paid ten times as much! But, of course, there's something wrong here – the meaning of the term 'responsible' gets changed half way through: in the first case, 'responsible for it' means 'doing it', but in the second case, 'responsible for it' means 'seeing that it gets done'.

Let me suggest that supervisory responsibility was instituted as a checks-and-balance sort of thing, as a quality control mechanism. And this is a good thing. But having someone be responsible for making sure another person does his/her job is quite different than having that someone be responsible for the other person's job.

And the first kind of responsibility need not have a great deal more status and salary attached to it. In fact, it need not have *any* more status and salary attached to it. A doing X, B doing Y, C doing Z, and D double-checking A, B, and C doing X, Y, and Z – why shouldn't all four people be considered equal in terms of status and salary? In fact, one could argue that A, B, and C should have more status and salary than D. It usually takes more skill and effort to *do* X, Y, and Z, to a standard than to see whether they got done to that standard. And if B messes up, why can't B be held responsible for not doing Y, and D held responsible for not checking B's work (which is different from D being held responsible for not doing Y)? And why can't B have control over how to do Y, and D have control over how to check B doing Y (which is different from D having control over B)? There would be a need for B's work to be accessible to D, but accessible is not the same as controllable. This way, both responsibility and control are kept in their proper spheres. And both B and D are treated like adults. And neither is put on a fast track to an ulcer. (Of course, another arrangement is to have A doing X, B doing Y, C doing Z, and A double-checking B, B double-checking C, and C double-checking A; no need for D at all.)

So why does the corporate world maintain the problematic view of responsibility? Well, it sure keeps the hierarchy cemented in place. The very terms 'subordinate' and 'superordinate' mean 'inferior' and 'superior' (in fact, one often hears references to 'one's superiors' rather than, as is more accurate, 'one's *organizational* superiors'). So my guess is that the desire to control is not necessarily linked to responsibility;

more often, it's linked to ego.

Leadership?

Some time ago, I attended a "Women in Leadership" conference put on by one of Ontario's larger unions. What I learned there disillusioned two parts of me: the labour part and the feminist part.

In the seminar on Collective Bargaining, I was told that "Every negotiation is an exercise in perceived power: if you have power and act as if you don't, then you don't; if you don't have power and act as if you do, then you do." If you don't have power, then don't act as if you do! Don't act like every obnoxious male I know, strutting about with an inflated sense of importance, acting like The Authority on Everything. Yes, of course, many buy the act (including, eventually, the actor): many are suckered in by the suit and tie, the bass voice speaking with weighty pauses, the overly serious demeanour. But to pretend is to deceive. And to pretend in order to gain power, in order to control – that's manipulation.

Furthermore, I'm disturbed by the view that perception is more important than reality. Although perception may well guide human action more often than reality, I think that that state of affairs is unfortunate. Whatever happened to 'Don't judge a book by its cover'? To perpetuate, indeed to encourage, pretence over substance, form over content, is very dangerous. Especially at the bargaining table. It occurred to me that the union probably hires image consultants – does it pay them more than it does its policy consultants?

I was also told that "*I need* is better than *I want*." Wait a minute, there is a difference between needs and wants, and to call a want a need is misleading, and, again, manipulative. So is inflating needs and wants, the next piece of advice.

I was reminded of the scene in Ayn Rand's *Atlas Shrugged*

in which a worker describes why the fictional socialist-run Twentieth Century Motor Company failed miserably: at first 'from everyone according to their abilities, to each according to their needs' worked fine, but then people didn't just need supper for their kids and a wheelchair for their grandmother, they needed cream for their coffee, they needed the living room replastered, and they needed a new car. Well of course it was the squeaky wheels (the "rotten, whiny, snivelling beggars") that got the grease – as well as the yacht they 'needed'.

It's hard enough to reach an agreement when two parties have different objectives; to lie about those objectives makes it harder, not easier. We should say what we mean and mean what we say. So if you want X, say you want X, not X times two. It's the morally correct thing to do, but even from a pragmatic point of view, it makes sense: people stop believing people who exaggerate, people who lie.

"Negotiations is a game." One seminar leader said it, and another illustrated it. The 'ice breaker' in her seminar was a game called "Diverse Points". Basically the game went like this: the Leisure Area was for single players to form pairs in preparation for negotiation; the Negotiations Area was for negotiation – people met in pairs and tried to reach agreement on how to divide 100 points between them in any of four proportions, 90/10, 80/20, 70/30, 60/40 (a division of 50/50 was not permitted); the object of the game was to accumulate as many points as possible and the player with the highest total score was the winner.

Well. First of all, trying to get as many points as possible is not negotiating, it's competing.

Second, why isn't a split of 50/50 permitted? In the absence of significance (the points had no meaning) and, therefore, rationale, a split of 50/50 is, to my mind, most fair. Why structure a game that excludes fairness as a possibility? Could it be that achieving fair agreement is not the point?

Third – the Leisure Area! I suppose it was intended to simulate the golf course, the tennis court, the cocktail lounge – you butter up your associate, pretending to be friends, doing the leisure thing together, and then you saunter over to the Negotiations Area. 'How To Use Your Friends' couldn't be written more clearly over the entrance. Instead, why not just show up at the Negotiations Area when you want to negotiate?

I played the game, with great reluctance and after considerable thought, trying to average 50 points per negotiation. As I mentioned earlier, it was the best I could do in terms of fairness (I believe a split of 90/10 could also be fair – it depends on context, which was absent). To my pleasant surprise, many of the women I interacted with were quite happy with this approach, and we easily and pleasantly decided who would get 40 and who would get 60, based on each of our totals so far; sometimes we agreed on 70/30, or even 80/20, if one of us was quite a bit over an average of 50 and the other quite a bit under. However, at least one woman lied to me about her point average. This was not surprising, given the preceding instruction. She may have been the winner, I'm not sure; to be honest, I didn't care much who won.

The conference proceeded and the more I learned about succeeding in my role as a union officer, as a woman on the labour front, the more I wished I hadn't been elected by my branch. The last thing I remember was this statement: "Collective bargaining has nothing to do with logic or reason." Apparently it has nothing to do with ethics either.

Crossing the Line

I crossed a picket line once. The Ontario Federation of Secondary School Teachers (OSSTF) in the Toronto area was on strike in 1983, and one of their demands was that union members be hired to fill night school and summer school teaching positions. They were concerned about quality of education: they didn't want these courses to become second-class courses as a result of being taught by second-class teachers who were unqualified and inexperienced.

Well. I was qualified. More qualified than many of the older OSSTF members who got their teaching jobs when you didn't even need a B.A., let alone a B.Ed. And I was experienced. In addition to about ten years of private music and dance teaching experience, I'd had a half-time regular day school position for one year and had taught a few night school courses the following year.

But more than that, I was enraged: what right does a person who already has a full-time teaching job and income (a wage that even at the lowest point is enough to support *two* people) have to an extra, a second, teaching job and income when there are so many without even a first?

Insofar as unions fight against abuses by management, I support them. It's the have-nots pulling together against the haves. But more and more today, union members themselves are the haves – they have jobs. And when they take action to protect (only) their own members, as is their mandate, well, it's the same old us/them thing, isn't it? And it perpetuates, it doesn't eradicate, class inequality.

If unions really want to honour their socialist history, they'd not be selfishly protecting their own but sharing. At the time, in Canada, about one in ten was unemployed. If those nine employed people had given up just four hours of their forty-hour work week, that tenth could've been employed – and all ten would have a very adequate thirty-six hours a week income.

There's something morally indecent about expecting the have-nots to support the haves, asking them to forego the little bit of income they could get as replacement workers (I prefer the term 'bandages' to 'scabs') in support of fringe benefits and pension plans for the regular workers. Pretty soon, unions will be asking the people in Thailand and wherever not to accept the jobs at Mattel and GM. And *that's* crossing the line. [1]

---

1. Of course, one has to consider population control as well: if you're reproducing yourself for no good reason and I'm not, why should part of my job go to your offspring? That is, why should your choices reduce my quality of life?

Mentoring: It's Who You Know

Studies show that people who have had mentors, who have had someone to provide "sponsorship, exposure, visibility, coaching, protection, and challenging assignments – activities which directly relate to the protégé's career" do indeed experience more career advancement than people who have not had mentors [1]. In a study of 1241 American executives, 67% of all respondents said they had a mentor [2]. Which just goes to show – it's who you know. That's how, why, they *are* executives.

Given that it's a 1979 statistic, presumably the respondents are referring to an informal mentorship, which arises spontaneously, as opposed to a formal mentorship, which is arranged by the organization as part of a mentoring program. The problem in both cases, however, is that most people who are in a position to mentor, a position of power and prestige, a well-connected position, are men. Still. So sexism keeps women from becoming protégés – because even if the guy's wife is fine with it, everyone will wonder whether she's sleeping her way to the top and that'll handicap her, essentially cancelling any advantage of the mentorship. Furthermore, women who could be mentors avoid mentoring other women because they fear being labelled feminist troublemakers. Why don't men avoid mentoring other men for fear they'll be labelled – what, part of the old boys' network?

All that aside, it seems to me that mentoring is unfair: it makes 'it's who you know not what you know' true. Merit becomes *not* the sole criterion for advancement.

Though perhaps mentoring counters chance. Chance is unfair too. With mentoring, those who do get doors opened for them are those who deserve it. But to say 'All A are B' doesn't mean 'All B are A': to say 'All those who are mentored have merit' doesn't mean 'All those with merit become mentored'. I'm not sure mentors choose their protégés according to merit (or develop merit in their protégés). (In which case, mentoring simply legitimizes favouritism. [3])

So why *do* mentors choose who they choose? Why do mentors mentor at all? I wonder if it isn't just some primitive lineage impulse in action. You know ... men need a son, someone to carry on the family name. And since it's more and more unlikely that men have *actual* sons in a position to be their protégés ... Do mentors tend to choose sons of friends when available? Do they tend to choose people who are twenty to thirty years younger, in the 'son' age bracket? What about women who mentor? More likely, *their* motive is social justice [4], not personal legacy.

I'm not saying people shouldn't seek, or give, advice and guidance. But a mentor doesn't just act as a source of information about the policies and procedures of the organization, help you with specific skills, give you feedback, etc. A mentor often does *more* than that: a mentor introduces you to influential people in the organization, facilitates your entry to meetings and activities usually attended by high-level people, publicly praises your accomplishments and abilities, recommends you for promotion, and so on. But see here's the thing. Introductions should be unnecessary. Meetings attended by high level personnel shouldn't be open to others. *Everyone's* accomplishments and abilities should be praised publicly. Only your immediate supervisor or some named designate should be able to recommend you for a promotion. And so on.

So the need for mentors means the organization isn't structured to advance based on merit. So shouldn't mentors' efforts instead be directed to making sure that it is? To making sure that mentors aren't needed? You shouldn't need a mentor to open doors because the doors shouldn't be locked. You shouldn't need a mentor to give you inside information because there shouldn't be any inside information: an organization's policies and procedures should be written out for all to read, perhaps even presented at a new employee training session (and there should be no unwritten policies, no under-the-table procedures); any preferences for application materials, be it for a job, a promotion, or a grant, should be stated on the application form itself, or perhaps explained in a separate 'Tips for Applicants' sheet; and knowledge of any available job, promotion, or grant should be freely accessible to all. Influential people should use their influence only in formal channels; their authority should only be that vested in them by the terms of their job description.

Men are so proud of not mixing pleasure and business, of separating the personal from the public. Bullshit. Aren't a lot of critical connections, let alone decisions, made on the golf course? At the bar? Between conference sessions? It seems that by 'personal' and 'pleasure' they just mean women – wives, daughters, sexual liaisons. They leave the women in their lives out of consideration. But their relationships with their buddies and their sons – these are very much brought into the workplace.

---

1. "Formal and Informal Mentorships: A Comparison on Mentoring Functions and Contrast with Non-mentored Counterparts," Georgia T. Chao and Pat M. Walz *Personnel Psychology* 45.3 (1992)
2. "Much Ado about Mentors," B. Roche. *Harvard Business* Review 5.7 (1979)
3. Or its opposite: let's not forget that mentors can close doors too – what do you do when your mentor starts 'forgetting' to 'mention' you?
4. For example, several mentoring programs are designed for women and minorities *because* they are unconnected, because they are "not as well integrated into departmental or institutional networks" (Linda K. Johnsrud, "Enabling the Success of Junior Faculty Women through Mentoring" in *Mentoring Revisited: Making an Impact on Individuals and Institutions*, p.53). But this just compensates for an unfair system; it doesn't make it less unfair.

Unprofessional

As in 'unprofessional behaviour' or 'unprofessional attire'. As in 'not good'. As in 'cause for dismissal'. Given that extreme consequence, we'd better define 'unprofessional'. Easier said than done.

The word 'professional' means, simply, 'pertaining to the profession'. Not helpful. Let's assume that the profession's *standards* are being referred to, standards which, presumably, identify a certain minimum regarding *quality of performance*. For example, good counselling depends on trust; specifically, for example, the counsellee trusts the counsellor not to tell others what has been discussed during the session. Therefore, a counsellor who fails to maintain confidentiality is being unprofessional. As another example, it is incontestable that certain professions are best carried out when their practitioners do not accept bribes. So if a police officer or a lawyer does accept a bribe, s/he would be guilty of unprofessional behaviour. So far, so good.

What about the professor who has a relationship with a student? *Is* it incontestable that university education is best achieved *without* personal attachment between professor and student and/or when the professor is impartial? Is impartiality possible, let alone probable, even *without* professor-student relationships? (I'm thinking of racial, religious, and gender prejudices, and even simple personality conflicts.) And do personal attachments necessarily mean *lack of* impartiality?

Consider the profession of broadcast journalism. One could argue that based on the evidence of public opinion polls, a newscast is taken more seriously (i.e., is more successful) when delivered in a bass voice. So it would be unprofessional to hire tenors, let alone altos and sopranos.

Things become even murkier when we leave unprofessional behaviour and venture into unprofessional attire. In which professions is the success of the job dependent on specific attire? Incontestably, scuba diving and fire fighting. What about nursing? Why do they have to wear those uniforms? They aren't intrinsically sterile. Ease of identification in emergencies? Okay, I'll accept that. What about the staff at fast food outlets? I should think correct identification is pretty much guaranteed by their being behind the counter (not that getting fries with that is a matter of any urgency). From here, we can readily get into the ridiculous: how does wearing lipstick and mascara relate to success on the job for an airline worker or a bank teller? (One of the former was fired for not wearing any make-up, one of the latter for wearing too much.) How does wearing cotton pants and a sweatshirt relate to success on the job for an elementary school teacher? (Suspended without pay for the entire school year.)

That much of professionalism is concerned with appearance is unsettling for several reasons:

(1) There is often no correspondence between the appearance of competence and competence itself; whether that teacher wears polyester or denim, for example, does not, *can*not, indicate the quality of her teaching. (Especially in education, this view is abhorrent because it contradicts one of the fundamentals of scientific inquiry: we try to teach our students to understand what it *is*, not what it *looks* like.)

(2) It violates one of our moral fundamentals – 'Don't judge a book by its cover' and 'It's what's on the *inside* that counts' – and makes us hypocrites.

(3) Accordingly, it doesn't matter then whether or not we actually *do* X; it matters only whether or not it *looks like* we've done X. Hello?

Truth is, much of professionalism comes down to custom. The airline attendant was not conforming to custom. Nor was the bank teller. Nor the teacher. Each was doing something a little aberrant, a little individual. But how can we justify equating 'professionalism' with 'conformity'? (Well, we seem to equate *'morality'* with 'conformity' fairly easily …) A researcher was once reprimanded for using 'unprofessional salutations' in letters requesting information: rather than 'Dear Sir/Madam', a simple 'Hi' began the letter. Unprofessional or just unconventional? Would recipients of such letters really refuse to send the information just because 'Dear Sir/Madam' wasn't used? (What do we take each other for?)

Now, from 'doing what's expected' (custom), we easily get to 'doing what you're told' (obedience) as a definition of professionalism. Consider this, from a biography by Vicki Goldberg: " … she did not seek out politically charged stories to make her political point, nor refuse an assignment for political reasons (or for any other). *Margaret was a professional*" (my emphasis). In fact, it may not be unusual for charges of 'unprofessionalism' and 'insubordination' to occur together (insubordination referring, of course, to not deferring to your supervisor, perhaps especially with respect to orders given).

In fact, it's beginning to look like being professional is incompatible with being an individual, an individual with ideas, values, thoughts, feelings, integrity. To be professional, you wear a uniform (you look like everyone else, you become *im*personal) and you do what you're told (you listen to another person, rather than to your own person). Is it not 'unprofessional' for a doctor to refuse to help an injured person who has just killed and is certain to kill again? No doubt, it would be 'unprofessional' for an engineer to refuse a project with military applications. Impartiality and emotional distance, no personal opinions or judgements – I'd say professionalism is downright dangerous.

Ethics without Philosophers
(the Appalling State of Affairs in Business)

Could someone without a business degree become a marketing consultant? Then how is it that people without philosophy degrees are becoming ethics consultants? [1] Is it that people don't know that Ethics is a branch of Philosophy just as Marketing is a branch of Business? Doubtful. Is it just the typical male overstatement of one's expertise? [2] Perhaps. Is it that people think they already know right from wrong, they learned it as children, there's really no need for any formal training in ethics? Possible. I have certainly met that attitude in business ethics classes and ethics committees. [3] Or is it that ethics consultants (advisors, officers, practitioners, and so on) don't really act as consultants about ethics? They act as consultants about managing ethical behaviour. Actually, they don't even do that. Ethical consultants, practitioners, officers, focus on how to increase the likelihood that employees will follow some specific professional code of ethics or, more likely, the ethical rules the company's elite want them to follow. They don't, as they proclaim, 'develop methodologies for ethical decision-making.' [4] [5]

As far as I can see, business ethics courses taught by business faculty and ethics programs run by managers are is superficial at best. [6] First, following a code if just an appeal to custom, an appeal to tradition, which philosophers consider a weak basis, if not an actual error in reasoning: just because it's common to do it that way doesn't mean it's right; just because you've always done it that way doesn't mean it's right.

Second, legal moralism is prevalent: if it's legal, it's right, and if it's not illegal, it's not wrong. Few philosophers (and I daresay few intelligent people) accept this equivalence of moral rightness and legality. After all, slavery was once legal, and even at that time many considered it wrong and had excellent arguments to support their position (which is, to some extent, why the law changed – ethics should determine law, not the other way around).

Third, the so-called 'media test' and 'gut test' are essentially nothing but appeals to intuition, which is nothing more than childhood conditioning that makes us say X 'feels' wrong. I think it far better to approach ethical issues with thought, to consider the many rational approaches to making decisions about right and wrong, such as an appraisal of values, principles, consequences, and so on.

A second weakness of ethics as done by non-philosophers is that what takes place is usually preaching not teaching. That is, course material consists of 'This is the right thing' and 'Do this in this situation' – professors simply convey the current conventions and standard practices and legal obligations. The underlying principles and values are unexamined, and likely to be inadequate or contradictory in any case.

The human resources director or management executive is simply not equipped to examine the principles and values enshrined in the code she or he advocates [7], nor to approach an ethical issue with any rigor (for example, to figure out whether affirmative action programs are really fair, to determine if a proposed advertising campaign is really coercive, or to decide if anticipated environmental destruction is ethically justifiable), let alone teach various ways of making decisions about right and wrong.

Philosophers are. Not only are they equipped to approach ethical issues with rigor, they look at the principles and values involved in such approaches; they would consider whether one should conform to the codes that are so taken for granted by those in business, whether those codes are at all adequate. A philosopher's focus is thus more fundamental. And therefore prerequisite. That's why the business ethics done by non-philosophers is so alarming: it's building a house without a foundation – or, rather, convincing people to live in the house, without examining the foundation.

A very rudimentary version of a philosopher's methodology for ethical decision-making would be something like this:
1. Identify the ethical issue, the question to be answered.
2. Identify the relevant facts, consulting all involved.
3. (a) Identify the relevant moral principles and values.
   (b) Rank them.
4. (a) List all the decision options.
   (b) Identify the consequences for each option.
5. Align the options with the values and principles – which are upheld, which are violated?
6. Decide what is the 'rightest' thing to do.
7. Repeat the process for deciding about the 'rightest' way of doing it.

I present below notes that I made (while I served on the ethics committee of a local hospital) for analysis of ethical problems to show what a philosophically trained person can do:

I. A Nephrology Questionnaire was presented to the committee by Dr. X for approval.

The basic question underlying the questionnaire is this: *Who gets dialysis?*

This question can be framed as
(1) a futile treatment question
(2) an allocation of resources question

The first has already been discussed, the main issues being the definition of 'futile' and whether we have a moral obligation to provide futile treatment.

With regard to the second, decisions can be made according to the following three criteria:

i) *medical value* in prolonging life, alleviating pain, and/or enhancing life – key questions are 'How much value?' and 'How likely is the value to be achieved?' and the central conflict would be between the 'best outcome' approach (an end point approach) and the 'most in need' approach (a beginning point approach)
ii) *self worth* – the key question here is 'Does the person have a high or low quality of life?' (and is a subjective standard or an objective standard used to determine this?)
iii) *social worth* – the key question here is 'Does the person contribute to or cost society?' (this would include consideration of emotional and/or economic dependents)

These three criteria can be used
- *simultaneously* (consider all three at the same time)
- *serially* (if, and only if, the first criterion is met – that is, the dialysis does have
medical value – is the next criterion considered)

These three criteria can be given *equal* or *different* weight. One can judge
- according to *consequences* (in which case the 'best outcome' might weigh heavily, but one would have to ask outcome for who – the patient only, or for the family, or for society as a whole)
- according to *rights* (do all have equal rights to the treatment, in which case we toss a coin or consider 'first come, first served')
- according to *justice* (are some more deserving than others?)

One can also, of course, combine these approaches: for example, a person might by lifestyle forfeit their rights and so another might be more deserving.

By way of contrast, non-philosophically trained people (the others on the ethics committee) would've responded with something like 'I think the questionnaire's okay' or 'I think it's too long.' See the difference?

Here's another example:

II. Dr. Y was faced with a request by a mother to employ aggressive management for her newborn son whose longevity was limited (following a premature birth and surgery for a severe fetal anomaly).

I identified six ethical issues involved the decision faced by Dr. Y:

(1) the conflict between physician and patient/proxy issue:
• the physician can override patient/proxy requests in some circumstances, one of which is a request for futile treatment, another of which is a request for harmful treatment unbalanced by benefit; this may be especially defensible if the proxy has already made an ethically questionable decision (in this case, the decision to carry to term with full knowledge of the defect)
objection: patient/proxy requests must always be fulfilled
response: this position simply seems indefensible

(2) the futile treatment issue:
 (i) the aggressive management requested falls into the category of futile treatment (the procedures won't cure the condition)
 (ii) the aggressive management won't prolong life - and if it does, such life is of insufficient quality (must define 'insufficient', perhaps by reference to mental abilities, physical abilities, and presence of pain) and/or the prolonging is too short-term to be worthwhile (must define 'worthwhile', perhaps as above)
 (iii) the aggressive management won't alleviate pain
objection: the procedures would alleviate the parents' pain

response: this would be using the baby as a means to others' end; such alleviation doesn't override lack of benefit to the baby; such alleviation doesn't override harm to the baby
objection: life should be maintained at all costs in all cases
response: this position is indefensible
(3) the harmful treatment issue:
• the aggressive management falls into the category of harmful treatment unbalanced by benefit because there is physical trauma involved and/or because there is no resulting recovery, minimal prolonging (quality and quantity), and/or minimal alleviation of pain
(4) the DNR issue:
• the physician should (a) make a DNR order (b) against the proxy's wishes
• re (a), arguments re futile treatment apply
• re (b), arguments re conflict apply
• also, proxies don't have medical expertise
• also, proxies are biased by love/emotion
objection: the parents bear the consequences the most
(5) the euthanasia issue:
• the physician should (a) provide euthanasia (b) against the proxy's wishes
• re (a) and (b), if the patient is in pain, especially/but only (?) serious pain, which is resistant to alleviation and/or there is no hope of recovering to a certain quality of life (must define 'certain' perhaps as above with 'insufficient')
• re (b), if the proxy's wishes are clearly not in the patient's best interests (in this case, we can't use the 'patient's previously expressed wishes' standard, nor the 'patient's would've expressed wishes' standard)
objection: life should be maintained at all costs in all cases
response: this position seems indefensible
objection: passive, but not active, euthanasia is acceptable

response: there is no difference if the motive, intention, and consequence are the same
objection: euthanasia is illegal in Canada
response: ethics overrides legalities
(6) the allocation of resources issue:
• probably doesn't apply in this case, but if it does, it seems merely to strengthen most of the preceding arguments (rather than add any)
Recommended reading:
Defective Newborns" Michael D. Bayles
"Selective Nontreatment of Handicapped Newborns" Robert F. Weir

By way of contrast, non-philosophically trained people would've responded with something like 'I think you should do what the mother has asked you to do, after all, she's the mother' or 'I think you should do whatever is in the baby's best interest.' Again, see the difference? These responses are no different than, no better than, what the physicians would've gotten in the lunch room. (Which is why they brought the matters to the ethics committee!)

To see similar differences in business, one need only compare business ethics articles with papers written by philosophers. The philosophers will deal, in depth, with any one of a number of difficult issues; for example, if the issue is advertising, she or he might investigate the various kinds and degrees of influence and deception; the rights of persons to be free from intrusions in their physical, sonic, and visual space; the difference between private and public space; the special rights of children given their undeveloped cognition; the relevance of what's advertised and how it's advertised; and so on. The managers will present a checklist for making sure their marketing campaigns don't break any laws. The former will contain arguments, the latter mere assertions.

How has this terrible misunderstanding, this doing ethics without philosophers, come about? Perhaps the problem lies with the term 'applied ethics'. Business people take it to mean applying ethical codes, setting up policies and procedures that conform to – well, there's the problem: that conform to *which* ethics? (And perhaps only a philosopher would ask this question.)

Or perhaps the problem is that philosophers have understood 'applied ethics' to mean applying ethical analyses – identifying and examining the ethical issues in business. Because 'ethics' doesn't mean 'moral rules'; 'ethics' means *'the study of* moral rules'. This is a common misunderstanding. A term with a very specific meaning among specialists has been adopted and used erroneously in the general population. [8]

But I can't help wondering if it hasn't just been a case of blatant appropriation. Business has hijacked ethics as a marketing tool, just as it did with environmentalism, and turned it into something superficial and useless. Managers aren't really not interested in the substantial, fundamental matters. They just want a new way to attract customers and clients and so increase profits. Indeed the blurb for an ethics seminar titled "Integrity Wins", offered by and for ethics practitioners, not philosophers, described its purpose as "explor[ing] how ethical issues ... can affect the legal status, revenue generation, and perceived trustworthiness of your organization." A subscription form for *The Corporate Ethics Monitor* says this:

"Successful executives, investor relations professionals, and independent corporate directors understand that business ethics is not a fad. They know why companies are beefing up their ethical management, training and compliance programs. They understand that high-profile misconduct can cause serious repercussions for a company – including alienation of customers, suppliers, employees, investors and business partners. Therefore, quite apart from a desire to avoid fines and other financial penalties resulting from ethical problems, an effort to identify potential points of ethical weakness can pay off in higher morale and productivity, an enhanced reputation, and a healthier bottom line."

Nothing is said about doing the right thing *because* it's the right thing!

However, I don't want to put the blame solely on business. If philosophy faculty didn't have such disdain for business, and if they took a little responsibility for their discipline, there would be more preparation for philosophy majors to *be* ethics practitioners. Philosophy departments should advise their students of careers as ethics officers and consultants; they should encourage their students to, therefore, take courses in business (if they want to become a business ethics officer) or science (if they want to become ethics consultants in bioethics or environmental ethics), because without a background in business or science, philosophers won't know which questions to ask, what difficulties to anticipate (for example, ethical belief in intercultural business is a real thorny issue – philosophy students will have to grapple with moral relativism in a big way ...). Philosophy departments could even arrange to have their applied ethics courses team-taught; this would require business, similarly, to dampen their disdain for philosophy.

---

1. I have only anecdotal information here. I did send a three-item questionnaire to survey the Ethics Officer Association (U.S.), the Ethics Practitioners Association of Canada, and the Canadian Center for Ethics and Corporate Policy. In the first case, I was informed they have no way to track the education status of their members as that was not one of the questions asked on their membership application, and apparently they were not interested in sending my three questions to their members; in the second case, again, I don't think my questions got passed on; in the third case, my questions did get passed onto the Board of Directors, but no further, and I received three replies –

one person had a B.A. in Science and an M.B.A., another indicated that he was a Chartered Accountant, and the third had a B.A. and an LL.B. with no particular training in ethics.

2. My personal experience strongly indicates that most ethics consultants are men.

3. Though, of course, childhood ethics doesn't tell you who gets the kidney and at what price.

4. I say that developing methodologies for ethical decision-making surely refers to decision-making that accords with the company code because methodologies for ethical decision-making already exist, (Are ethics practitioners intending to reinvent or surpass Aristotle, Kant, Mill, McIntyre, and the many, many others who have developed ways to determine what is right? Doubtful.)

5. And yet even at this rudimentary level, they fail. Perhaps the biggest obstacles to ethical behaviour are bonuses for behaviour that increase profit. Dangling such a carrot in front of someone for doing the profitable thing makes it harder, not easier, to do the right thing. High salaries, which will be lost if one loses one's job, which will happen if one doesn't increase profit, is another way exactly *not* to 'encourage compliance'. So of course if a company were really serious about their ethics, they'd give bonuses for doing the right thing, whether or not profit is increased or decreased.

6. Of all the conferences I've attended, only for the ethics practitioners conference was I told what to wear. Philosophers don't care; they understand it's not important.

7. Consequently, ethical codes remained unexamined and, therefore, more often than not, useless. Partly, this is because there is no definition: what exactly is professionalism, for instance? Excellence? Integrity? The last-mentioned, so often listed as a value in codes of ethics, is nothing more than non-hypocrisy: having integrity means that if you think X is right, you should *do* X. It doesn't indicate *what* is right in the same way that, for example, honesty or beneficence does. Examination reveals that transparency and accountability are similar to integrity. I've even seen 'objective' [sic] [not 'objectivity'] listed in a code of ethics – again, qualified attention to definition would reveal that objectivity isn't a moral value.

And partly ethical codes are useless because of internal conflict and lack of prioritization. For example, one code I looked at says employees "shall act in a manner that is in the best interests of their clients and employer consistent with the public interest." That one item alone is fraught with internal conflicts. It doesn't take a genius to imagine an instance in which the best interests of the client *collide with* the best interests of the employer, let alone the public interest. When they collide, when, for example, honesty conflicts with loyalty, or providing the highest quality of service conflicts with providing the highest return to shareholders, which one is to take precedence? The code doesn't say. I've seen *no* code of ethics provide a means of ranking values, a means of resolving such conflicts.

8. The term 'philosophy' is itself is another example: to philosophers, it means something like the critical examination of fundamental concepts, but to the general population it means simply a certain view of or attitude toward life.

Why Teaching Business Ethics can be Difficult

Teaching a business ethics course can be more difficult than one anticipates. This is so for a number of reasons, which are briefly outlined below. The list is not necessarily unique to business ethics – some of these problems apply to other courses as well, particularly other applied ethics courses. And, very importantly, some of these problems also apply to the teaching one does as an ethics consultant or an ethics officer serving on an ethics committee or in an ethics program.

1. *You're a philosophy professor.* Know that both inside and outside academia, philosophy doesn't have a very good reputation. [1] (Indeed, 'academic' doesn't have a good reputation. The word is often used in the business world to dismiss something as irrelevant – 'Yes, well, the question's academic, isn't it.') Philosophy is typically considered useless or easy. Or both. Since it's useless, you'll never have your students or committee members/employees' attention. Since it's easy, you'll never have their full effort. And when your students receive a grade they were not expecting (usually that'd be anything less than an 'A'), they'll be outraged. And likely very vocal about it.

A solution to this problem might be to team teach the course with a business professor.

2. *You're teaching to non-philosophy majors.* Philosophy majors tend to understand, or learn pretty quickly, that philosophy is more, not less, difficult than other disciplines (top scorers on the GRE tend to be philosophy majors or physics majors – they are the ones most adept at critical, abstract reasoning), so they pay close attention and work hard. Non-philosophy majors tend to think (as mentioned above) that philosophy is a 'bird' course. [2] So (as

mentioned above) they won't work very hard and yet will be outraged to receive a poor grade.

It might help to present the GRE stats. But don't just tell them. They won't believe you, you're just a philosophy prof. Give them your source:
http://www.umflint.edu/philosophy/phl-gre.htm
http://www.phil.stmarytx.edu/faculty/philhp/articles/gre.html
3. *You're teaching philosophy* – which typically involves the higher cognitive skills. To explain in terms of Bloom's taxonomy, while most business courses deal with knowledge and comprehension, and application, philosophy deals very much with the higher three levels – analysis, synthesis, and evaluation. If it's true that business students are typically the 'B' and 'C' students in high school (the 'A' and 'B' students go into science and humanities), then many of your students will simply not be up to it.

There are two important implications. First, abstraction is involved. Although the task is to *apply* the abstractions, the abstractions must nevertheless be dealt with. Principles and values must be understood and juggled (compared, evaluated, weighted). Business students (indeed, most people) are not comfortable with abstraction.

Second, evaluation is involved. You're requiring your students/participants to be critical. Most students, most people, have no training in critical thinking. And no, it doesn't come naturally.

Furthermore, your students/participants will misunderstand 'critical' – when you model the thinking you want them to develop, they will think you're being either needlessly negative or needlessly adversarial. They will not understand that being critical means simply evaluating the strength and weakness of an argument. They'll understand your critical approach as antagonistic, a personal attack.

They'll call you rude. They'll be offended. They'll accuse you of not respecting their beliefs. (And indeed you're not. Not without some support, some defence.) They'll complain to the Dean.

And the reason they will not understand that is because they will persist in thinking that everyone is entitled to their own opinion. They will not understand that some opinions are better than others. Because they will not understand the criteria for evaluation – they will not understand that there are rules of reasoning about which there is no 'matter of opinion'. For example, to conclude that because all A are B, all B are A is simply wrong – as wrong as concluding that 2 + 3 = 5. And it will come as a rude awakening to be told that they are simply wrong. [3]

What exacerbates all of this is that many assumptions have been presented as fact in the business program. For example, your students think the goal of business is to maximize profit. [4] Philosophers demand evidence for facts; they examine assumptions. And most of them can argue that ethics trumps profit. But say that in a room full of business students and most will tune you out and, so, fail the course. The others will become hostile [5]: they'll challenge you and spend a lot of time trying to win (most of your students will be male); they'll call you names and complain to the Dean that you don't respect their opinions. (And also fail the course).

It would help, of course, if Critical Thinking 101 were a prerequisite. If it's not, explain that *some opinions are better than others*: suggest that your students can express their opinion that Santa Claus exists until they're blue in the face, but until they present some reasons for their opinion, the rest of the class is justified in ignoring them (politely, of course); and until they present *good* reasons, the rest of the class is

justified in not changing its mind (assuming they disagreed).
4. *You're teaching ethics.* There are several implications of this.

First, people tend to think they already know right from wrong. After all, it's something we're taught as children. So, since you're not teaching them anything new, you won't get their attention or effort.

Further, since it *is* something we're taught as children, most people feel infantilized to be taught it as adults – and will resent it.

It might help to explain that ethically speaking, most of us are quite unsophisticated; we haven't updated our childhood. Most of our moral training stopped when we were somewhere around thirteen or fourteen years of age, but as adults, we have to deal with a lot of ethical issues that our childhood morality simply can't handle very well. It doesn't have much in the way of conceptual complexity and subtlety; it doesn't make the fine distinctions that are necessary; it's not as precise as it needs to be. For example, 'Do what your parents tell you' is fine until you realize that parents make mistakes too. 'Don't steal' is adequate as long as you're not starving and someone else has food that *they* have stolen. Even 'Do unto others as you would have them do unto you' must bite the dust: *you* may say 'tell me the truth' but some people really may prefer not to know – do you respect their wishes?

Just as someone who is educated about forestry can tell the difference between a five-year-old sick white pine and a ten-year-old healthy red pine (to me, they're all trees), and someone educated about colour can distinguish between magenta, scarlet, and burgundy (to you, they might all be red), someone *educated* about ethics will be able to distinguish between justified discrimination and unjustified discrimination or between morally acceptable profit and morally unacceptable profit. Those distinctions can then be used to make decisions.

Second, ethics is for girls. (Apparently.) And business is dominated by boys. It's Mom who teaches us right from wrong; she's the moral compass. And anything Mom does is to be held in contempt as soon as a boy hits puberty. In order to become a man, it's necessary. To hold in contempt all things female. Ethics presumes caring, and real men don't care. (Qualification: they don't care about others. They care about profit, their own place in the scheme of things, and because their sons are extensions of themselves, they care about them, *their* place in the scheme of things, but caring about strangers? Strangers are other; the other is the competition.) Ethics is something for priests to worry about and we all know priests aren't real men. They're celibate for gawdsake. So, men avoid ethics – it's effeminate to be concerned about right and wrong.

Third, despite the critical thinking element, in which there is a great deal of black and white, ethics is very 'grey'. Unlike many disciplines, there is typically no correct answer. In ethics, and ethics assignments, it's how you get the answer that is typically evaluated, not the answer itself. (See point 9, below.) Business students (and again, most people) [6] are uneasy, uncomfortable, with grey. They want black and white, a bottom line. (Which is why perhaps they cling to the bottom line of profit. It's easily quantifiable.) [6]

It might help to articulate and emphasize to your students before they become overwhelmed and give up that their goal is to become able to make *better* ethical decisions, more *carefully considered* decisions; they don't have to figure out with absolute certainty what's *right*, but just what's *better*.

Fourth, the subject matter is very sensitive. People will get upset; they will become disturbed. You are teaching what is perhaps the most sensitive course in the curriculum. No matter how carefully you lay the groundwork and say things like 'We're discussing positions/opinions, when someone criticizes a position, they're criticizing the position, not the person who holds that position, in fact we don't even need to know what positions you personally hold, that's your own business', there will be many students who don't have the maturity to handle a course that implicitly and explicitly questions the beliefs and values they hold dear. Their response is (further) resistance, anger, and hostility.

Fifth, morality is very personal. So people may respond with 'It's none of your business' when you try to elicit discussion. This is intensified in the workplace because there is this unfortunate assumption, belief, that one must leave one's personal life at the door.

5. *Writing skills become very important in business ethics courses* because students are typically required and write extended analyses of and arguments for various ethical positions. This kind of writing is very unlike the point form norm of business presentations (consider the standard of Power Point) and the expository short answer and multiple choice questions of business tests and exams. And most students aren't very good at it. (This is related to point 3, above.)

It would help if Business Communication 101 incorporated such writing.

6. *High level reading skills are required* since the student must be able to follow the extended reasoning typical of the text material; quite simply, the essays written by philosophers that rightly appear in many business ethics texts are *way* beyond business students.

7. *If the course (or participation in the program) is mandatory,* students (participants) will resent such coercion. This resentment will spill over.

8. *If the course (or participation in the program) is an elective,* students (participants) will assume that it's not, therefore, very important – certainly not integral to their business education, their job performance. Add this to the first point, that you're a philosophy professor, and you're truly fringe, so very *un*important. Being offered as an elective *every second year* sends a message of such unimportance, you may simply not be able to compensate. Give up.

9. *If you're a sessional instructor*, know that business students are very aware of rank. Hierarchy rules their world. So if you're 'just' a sessional, again, the course can't be very important or very difficult.

10. *If you teach the course in the evening*, see point 9.

11. *If you teach the course in a portable*, see point 9.

---

1. To be fair, humanities students don't think much of business either. The disdain is reciprocal. And yet I have a feeling that a course called "Marketing your Poetry Book" or "Running your Theatre" taught to humanities students by a marketing or management professor would be more attended to than the business ethics course taught to business students by a philosophy professor.
2. It takes a lot of work to critically evaluate a philosophy paper and maybe that's why so much bullshit gets an 'A' (supporting the students' opinion about philosophy courses) – professors simply become too tired to do a good job.
3. Formal logic and even informal logic courses attend to correct and incorrect reasoning.
4. So whether something is morally acceptable or not is simply irrelevant to them. It might come into play when two options yield the same profit, but how often does that happen? And even so, other concerns are likely to be tie-breakers.
5. Students become especially hostile when a lot of work is required for what is, after all, a 'bird' course. If they're used to knowledge and comprehension courses, then ethics, requiring arguments to support opinions, is doubly difficult. (And business students have led me to believe that the kind of critical and abstract thinking required

in these ethics courses is significantly different from anything they've had to do before – which worries me insofar as this kind of thinking, at a much more advanced level, is required for the Reading Comprehension and Logical Reasoning sections of the GMAT.)

6. This might be true especially of men. They gravitate toward the quantitative, the ill- (but sexually aptly-)named 'hard sciences' of engineering and chemistry, rather than the 'soft sciences' of psychology and sociology. They say such fields are not as legitimate, but really they're just harder to navigate because the reasoning and the evidence are 'stronger' and 'weaker' rather than 'right' and 'wrong'. (Which is why, when men *do* get involved with ethics, they prefer moral legalism, the approach that equates right and wrong with legal and illegal, which is black and white.)

Business Rules the World. Do we want it to?

One of the most common – and most serious – weaknesses of codes of ethics, and indeed, most ethical theories, is that they don't prioritize values. They're fine for many of the simpler ethical questions, but when goods and interests conflict, when virtues and rights collide, they don't provide a way to determine which interest, which right, is stronger. For example, it's all very nice to say that both customers and shareholders are valued, but which is valued *more*? Do you opt for lower prices or greater profits? And it's all very good to say that loyalty and honesty are among the company's virtues. But what does an employee do when honesty seems to be a breach of loyalty? Does the employee blow the whistle or not? The code I begin to develop here is an attempt to solve that problem, an attempt to prioritize values.

First, I propose that life be set in the position of highest priority: nothing is more valuable than life itself. This is so if only for logical reasons – without life, nothing else is possible, nothing else matters. A point of clarification: violations of this value, that is, the causing of death, need not be sudden or immediate: a slow poisoning is a poisoning nevertheless.

Included at this point, though perhaps better listed as a separate item so as not to be forgotten, would be the resources necessary to sustain life: food, water, and oxygen.

Having put life at the top, however, I hasten to explain that life for life's sake is not my aim. Rather, I see the value of life to be in its quality; life itself is a means to an end, the end being a certain quality of life. And I suggest, therefore, that freedom from pain and injury be also included.

Obviously, even to this point, there are questions I need to address. Just exactly which life forms am I including? I am a little uncomfortable specifying only *human* life, even though many other life forms are required *for* human life. But I am more uncomfortable including *all* life: the simplest construction project surely kills a few worms, and prohibiting such construction for that reason seems unwise. Where I draw the line is not clear to me at the moment. However, with respect to freedom from pain and injury, I include all sentient life: the presence of pain is worse than the absence of life for many creatures, especially those with fully developed pain receptors but little sense of time continuity and attendant life plans.

A further problem is that we often don't know for sure that someone is going to get killed. So probability must play a role. But, and here's the big question, how probable is probable enough? If there's a fifty-fifty chance that someone will get killed if X is done, is that a sufficient reason for choosing not to do X?

With respect to resources necessary to sustain life, one might well ask 'How much life?' Is it fair to say that the conduct of business must not diminish resources below the level required to sustain life while at the same time allowing life unlimited increase? I think not. Surely we can calculate the ideal quality of life we desire, and from that, calculate the ideal population level, given the nature (limits and renewability) of our resources. (I suspect these calculations have already been done, but since limiting population means limiting markets ...) Business must then not diminish the resources below the level needed to sustain that population.

Further, while in theory, the quantities of food, water, and oxygen necessary to sustain life are known amounts, ensuring these amounts is a difficult matter in practice. Since people are, at this moment, dying for lack of food and water, one might assume that we've already gone beyond the point of equilibrium. However, surplus food and water elsewhere on the planet suggests that the problem is one of distribution, not quantity.

With respect to freedom from pain and injury, one must ask 'How much pain and injury?' Specifying 'serious' solves little – 'How serious is serious?'

Further, given that all sentient life forms are included, one must ask whether they are also to be given equal consideration. That is, is a rat's pain of the same value as a human's pain?

And yet, even to this point, even with the most conservative answers to these questions, this code of ethics, if implemented, would radically change the face of business as we know it. Let me repeat that. *Even with the most conservative answers to these questions, this code of ethics, if implemented, would radically change the face of business as we know it.*

Before describing some of these changes, I'd like to append to my code two possibilities for veto. The first veto is that of voluntary and informed consent: if the person who is (probably) going to die or be injured is identifiable and s/he agrees to (the risk of) that death or injury, one is justified in carrying on with one's business. Proxy consent of non-human sentient life is not allowed, however.

The second veto involves the purpose of the business: if one is in the life-saving business, then perhaps some degree of life-taking is justified. Ditto for the business of life-sustaining resource production or the business of serious pain and injury alleviation – some 'taking in kind' may be allowed. The notion of sacrifice is difficult and beyond my objective at the moment, but I want to leave this door open: perhaps we can justify causing some pain, or even death, to some life forms, even of our own species, if we can thereby prevent a great deal of pain or save a great deal of lives.

Now, the application of my code so far is simple: barring the previous vetoes, no business decision that entails death, the destruction of life-sustaining resources, or serious injury is ethically justified. (See what I mean by radically changing the face of business ... .)

The implications of this code, however, are extensive: if the conduct of one's business entails someone's death, one should not conduct said business. No business is worth dying for. Even CEOs would (hopefully) agree. I expect the entire industrial revolution would have been considerably slower had this code been in use. Even today, some of the higher risk operations such as mining might be far less developed (and perhaps alternate energy sources would have been far more developed).

Further, if business-as-usual involves causing serious pain, one should not engage in such business-as-usual. No company's existence, let alone its profit margin, is worth another's pain, be it human or rodent. That is to say, almost any business involving animal experimentation would have to close. A fourth brand of dish detergent or eye mascara is simply not worth causing severe pain to even one rabbit. It is also to say that the military business would have to shut down. No more manufacture of 'anti-personnel missiles'.

And if the consequence is bankruptcy, so be it. Better that a company go bankrupt than that someone dies or gets seriously injured. (Note that *the company* does not have a right to life or to freedom from pain and injury.)

Further, assuming that we are already over the point of equilibrium with regard to life and resources, any business that is not environmentally-sustaining is ethically unjustified. That alone would have huge consequence.

Now at this point, I'd like to anticipate and respond to one objection. Closing down my business, one might argue, will involve a lot of negative consequences: thousands will be put out of a job, there will be no food on their tables, etc. To respond, I don't believe that a business closure has ever resulted in employee death or even serious pain and injury. When a company employs the whole town and it goes out of business, the town becomes a ghost town, yes, but because its people have moved on, not because they've died. Perhaps they are poorer, but better that some are poor than that some are dead. So, by my code, since life and freedom from pain and injury are ranked above having a job, the closure must be chosen if otherwise someone will die or get hurt.

The greatest result of implementing a code such as the one I propose might be, simply, the reduction of business. So many businesses provide services or products we simply don't need, or at least not in the quantity they're being produced, and as long as their production, in the process, violates this code (and I've just identified the first *three* values – I expect values four through whatever would include various freedoms and virtues that would further enhance quality of life), their very existence is unjustifiable.

With the reduction in business per se will come, hopefully, a marked decrease in its all-pervasive role in our lives. Nations are already just corporations; presidents and those who fill political offices are, more often than not, businesspeople – not philosophers, psychologists, sociologists, scientists ... Business rules the world. Do we *want* it to? *Do we really want someone's pursuit of profit to determine our lives?*

Change the way we do business

Looking back at the last fifty years, we see protests against deception and injustice: the anti-war movement, the civil rights movement, feminism, the gay rights movement, environmentalism, the animal rights movement, the Occupy movement. What's left? What should be the current generation's crusade? Big Business. Big Oil, Big Ag, Big Pharma, Big Media.

"In 2011, a think tank in London called the Carbon Tracker Initiative conducted a breakthrough study that added together the reserves claimed by all the fossil fuel companies, private and state-owned. It found that the oil, gas, and coal to which these players had already laid claim – deposits they have on their books and which were already making money for shareholders – represented 2,795 gigatons of carbon. ... [W]e know roughly how much carbon can be burned between now and 2050 and still leave us a solid chance (roughly 80%) of keeping warming below 2 degrees Celsius ... 565 gigatons. ... [A]s Bill McKibben [author of *Oil and Honey*] points out, 'The thing to notice is, 2,795 is five times 565. It's not even close. ... What those numbers mean is quite simple. This industry has announced, in filings to the SEC and in promises to shareholders, that they're determined to burn five times more fossil fuel than the planet's atmosphere can begin to absorb.' ... In other words, the fossil fuel companies have every intention of pushing the planet beyond the boiling point" (Naomi Klein, *This Changes Everything* 148, 353-4).

And Big Ag? "Billions of people on the planet are supported by farmers who save seeds from the crops and replant these seeds the following year. Seeds are planted. The crop is harvested. And the seeds from the harvest are replanted the following year. Most farmers cannot afford to buy new seeds every year, so collecting

and replanting seeds is a crucial part of the agricultural cycle. This is the way food has been grown successfully for thousands of years. With Monsanto's terminator technology, they will sell seeds to farmers to plant crops. But these seeds have been genetically-engineered so that when the crops are harvested, all new seeds from these crops are sterile (e.g., dead, unusable). This forces farmers to pay Monsanto every year for new seeds if they want to grow their crops." (Ethical Investing: Monsanto Terminator Technology
http://www.ethicalinvesting.com/monsanto/terminator.shtml

Big Pharma? The average price of the fifty drugs most used by senior citizens was nearly $1,500 for a year's supply. In 2002. And now they're creating the disease so they can sell the cure. Halitosis was just the beginning. Now we've got erectile dysfunction, female sexual dysfunction, bipolar disorder, attention deficit hyperactivity disorder (ADHD), restless legs syndrome, osteoporosis, social shyness (also called social anxiety disorder and social phobia), irritable bowel syndrome, and balding. We're all sick. We all need drugs. (Larry Dossey, "Creating Disease" *The Huffington Post* Jun18/10
http://www.huffingtonpost.com/dr-larry-dossey/big-pharma-health-care-cr_b_613311.html)

But this kind of information isn't screamed in the news because – Big Media. A mere six corporations own 90% of the median in the States.

So this is my call to this generation: protest against the veneer of respectability that has enabled 'business' to proceed 'as usual' – unchallenged. Question progress. Question profit. Question the right of way that's been given to business merely because it wears a suit and tie and provides jobs. 'I've got a business to run' is used as an all-purpose legitimizing excuse. As if merely by employing several people, business becomes some sort of social service. *It's not.*

You've got fifty years to learn from. The greater one's youthful idealism, the greater one's middle-aged bitterness. So, yes, many of us over forty are worse than useless: we are infectious with cynicism. But we were once young. Study what we did and what we didn't do. Figure out what worked and what didn't work – then. Figure out what'll work and what won't work – now. Take a good look at Kent State, Birmingham, Greenham Common, Tiananmen Square, Seattle … It's not as easy anymore (if it ever was) as offering a flower or sitting in the way. They will shoot you. They will run over you. And you can't depend on media coverage – your local station is owned by some fat cat in LA or NY who doesn't want the world to know. DIY. Use the internet. Figure it out.

As is the case with movements, little bits here and there gradually add up to something that makes the structure collapse and the veil of naïveté dissipate. Utopia doesn't rise from the rubble, but we never see things in quite the same way again.

A special note to those in business: with great power comes great responsibility. You're in the driver's seat. Get us out of here. Use your intelligence, use your imagination. Find a way. Change the way we do business. And save your world.

To Connect

Back when I was a teacher, I noticed a lot of incomplete sentences in my students' conversation and in their writing. But I thought hey, it's a fragmented world: videos with their bits and pieces of images, radio and TV with their sound bites, even entire degree programs present their courses as if they're unrelated.

But then I wondered, is it because they don't have complete thoughts or is it because they're used to being interrupted? If the latter, is that the cause or the effect? That is, were they interrupted so often they seldom got the chance to finish a sentence? So leaving sentences incomplete became a habit; worse, due to lack of practice, they never developed the ability to actually finish their sentences, to express complete thoughts. Or were they interrupting each other because they didn't expect an end, a complete sentence? In this case, they haven't really interrupted; I noted that they didn't even seem to consider it rude; it was just us older ones, those of us who *do* intend to finish our sentences, who felt interrupted.

Or, third possible explanation, was the incompleteness just the extreme of brevity? Apparently many students get through high school without having to write more than one paragraph on any give item. 'Extended thought? What do you mean?' Of course, in art, fragmented images are often effective. But unless the audience can make the implied connections, such art will also be unsuccessful. One study revealed that listeners didn't agree about whether a particular rap song condemned or condoned violence, suggesting that this is often the case.

Then I noticed that even when the sentences *were* complete, there were no connections *between* the sentences; there were no connections between paragraphs; there were entire essays without a thesis, without a point.

The problem isn't just the lack of continuity; it's the lack of *connection*. Connecting the dots makes something linear. Connecting them in a particular way gives the line a particular shape.

Call me masculist, call me eurocentric, but linear thought *is* important. The ability to connect enables us to survive. We need to see similarities and differences ("Categories", clap, clap, "Names of", clap, clap, "Colours" ...); we need to see cause and effect ("Look both ways before crossing ... ").

But my students' sentences lay like so many dots on a page. They expected *me* to make the connections, to give their work shape, to give it coherence. The most important words are not nouns or verbs: they're prepositions, conjunctions, and all the other transitional words – in, through, before, after, and, neither, therefore, because, although, despite. I actually had to spend time in a second year Philosophy class explaining that not only was 'A *because* B' not the same as 'A *therefore* B', but that they were exactly opposite.

It's not chance that left their writing without colons or semicolons. The former introduces an explanation or an example of a thought; the latter joins related thoughts of equal importance. If students don't see these connections between the dots, their sentences, they can't see, they have no use for, such advanced punctuation.

Further, when marking their papers, I often found myself writing 'wrong word' in the margin. This referred not to something like using 'quick' where one should use 'quickly' but to something like using 'with' where one should've used 'through'. Such an error indicates a fundamental lack of understanding of the connection, the relation, involved: 'A *with* B' describes merely a correlative relationship; 'A *through* B' can describe a causal relationship.

And 'irrelevant' and 'off-topic' – these are not just harmless 'messy bedroom' problems. Rather, something has been connected, albeit implicitly, without justification. This indicates that the person doesn't truly understand the nature of the subject and so can't tell if something is relevant or not.

My students seldom prepared an outline for their papers. ('What do you mean, an outline?') It wasn't a matter of laziness. And it wasn't a matter of just not bothering to write it out. Most often, the student didn't *know* what his/her main subjects were, and then what the subordinate subjects were for each of the main ones, etc. Preparing an outline is a rigorous task involving relation: chronological relation, causal relation, categorical relation, etc. Making an outline is making connections – *conceptual* connections. (I fear the best answer many would've given to 'Which doesn't belong – shoe, jacket, or saw?' is 'Jacket – because it doesn't begin with an S.')

But perhaps the scariest symptom, the most dangerous manifestation, of this inability to connect is the view that 'Everyone's entitled to their own opinion,' with its correlative, stated or implied, 'You can't criticize my opinion; my opinion is just as good as yours.' True enough if you didn't have to worry yourself with connections to fact (truth), or connections to other opinions (consistency), or connections to consequences (pragmatics). To understand that some opinions are better than others, some more certain, some more valuable, is one of the most important skills we can develop; but it is dependent on perceiving relations, on being able to connect.

The Absence of Imagination

We notice it when we say 'Kids don't know how to play anymore.' Gone are the games of dress-up and make-believe. The more specific and recognizable the toy, the more popular; least favourite are the ambiguous toys, the ones with so many possibilities.

Later, we observe and lament the fact that the students don't know how to amuse themselves. They can't sit quietly. Discipline problems abound. They are bored, school is boring, everything is boring. Their style becomes, necessarily, one of passivity. Or perhaps reactivity. But not proactivity – it takes imagination to initiate.

Why is this so? Why is there this absence of imagination? Perhaps because human beings are like most objects: we choose the path of least resistance. It takes less energy to watch TV than to read a book. It's easier to put on a prepared costume, use prepared props, and follow a prepared storyline than it is to make your own costume, props, and storyline. Sure, the latter is probably more satisfying. But how is the kid to know that if s/he hasn't experienced it? (And precisely *because* she hasn't experienced it, hasn't experienced the imagining, she can't imagine it.)

What to do? Anyone will tell you that forcing someone to do something is the quickest way to make them hate it. But given the contemporary context, it's unlikely the kid will voluntarily choose the seemingly less attractive and certainly less popular option.

And yet we'd better find a solution soon. As Céline says in *Journey to the End of the Night*, "Everything's allowed inside oneself." (He obviously wasn't a Roman Catholic, with its sick doctrine of sinful thoughts.) Using one's imagination is the perfect escape: anything goes and no one gets hurt. [1] People denied that escape route may be pushed to find another, less perfect one.

But not only might the unimaginative become the dangerous, the unimaginative becomes the deadweight: the unimaginative preschooler who becomes the bored (and boring) teenager becomes the useless adult. To improve, to change, requires that one *imagine* an alternative; in a thousand and one ways, our world is desperate for improvement, for change. But if we can't even imagine it, we sure as hell won't be able to make it happen.

My response to the ozone depletion, as one who read the biochemical facts and then gave up aerosols back in the 70s, was 'You can't say we didn't see it coming.' But I'm realizing, with more horror than accompanied my first conclusion (that 'we' were selfish, irresponsible, and just didn't give a damn), that 'we' *didn't* see it coming. We couldn't. People couldn't extrapolate from A to B: to anticipate the effect of a cause, the consequence of an action, requires imagination.

In the same way, I'm appalled to hear teenagers say what a good program it is that gives them a tour of jail or takes them into the operating room to see a gunshot wound. They 'didn't know', they say. *What?* What did you think happened when a bullet enters someone's body? Well, they didn't. They didn't think. They're not used to doing that. It requires a sort of 'let's pretend' mental activity that's simply not within their repertoire.

Ditto for the 'carrying the egg (or bag of flour) around for a week' exercise. I certainly didn't need to do that in order to understand what's involved in being a parent. And I'm the youngest child, so it's not like I saw it. *I imagined it.* I thought about what my life would be like if I had a child – and on that basis decided not to have one. Simple.

Apparently not. Imagination is necessary for the consideration of options, of alternatives; it's the prerequisite for choice, for exerting one's will, for having control over one's life. Without it, we are doomed, as individuals and as a species. It's what separates us (well, some of us) from lower life forms: if a horse could imagine life as a deer, my guess is it would jump the fence in a second. And while I'd like to say 'See ya', we're all in this together.

---

1. Ignoring for the moment that some research suggests that the more we imagine doing something violent, for example, the more we desensitize ourselves to it and more likely we become to actually do it.

Air Bands and Power Point

I still remember the feeling I had when I saw my first air band performance. It was a sick kind of feeling.

I hadn't known what an air band was. The announcement came over the P. A. at my school-for-the-day, and I dutifully shepherded the class to the gym. Then I watched, incredulous, as group after group of high school students came on stage and pretended to play their favourite songs. I mumbled a query to the teacher standing next to me. Apparently this air band stuff was quite big. Students spent weeks practising. They really wanted to get it right. 'It' being the appearance, the pretence.

In my day, the guys [sic] (sigh) actually *did* play, guitars and drums mostly. Each school had a couple bands. From time to time they even played at our dances.

But I tried not to go there. That was then, this was now. There is some skill required for this, I thought. It does take practice to get it right. But still. It bothered me. As everyone applauded – faking it.

I was reminded of that sick kind of feeling a few years later when I heard a new technopop piece on the radio; it was based on a sample from a Gene Krupa drum solo. That's how technopop is 'composed': someone uses bits and pieces ('samples') of other people's music and puts them together – often at random, mostly in repetition. That is to say, there's no coherent development, no substance.

It's sad to see that the ability to play, let alone compose for, a musical instrument is on the wane. But it's frightening to think about the why and the therefore.

I read somewhere that playing a musical instrument is the most mentally challenging task humans perform. Certainly the daily practice requires a level of both concentration and discipline that I just don't see anymore. Is it that our kids don't have the mental stamina needed to learn how to play a musical instrument? Or is it that because they don't learn how to play a musical instrument, they don't develop such mental stamina? Either way, it's cause for concern. And my guess is it's both.

That is to say, attention to pretence/form instead of to substance/content is both the cause and the effect of a paucity of higher cognitive skills. True, content without form can be incomprehensible. But form without content isn't anything at all. One must attend to content *before* one attends to form. At best, content *determines* form. Further, inattention to content entails inattention to *quality* of content. And that makes things so much worse.

Consider the addiction many people developed to the internet (even *before* social media sites). Surfing the net is like watching the news (and browsing the encyclopedia). It's kibbles and bits of information. That's all. It's pure content. Sure, it's knowledge. But is it *valuable* knowledge? Is it *relevant*, is it *sufficient*? Is it *usable*? One has to have some of those higher level cognitive skills to go beyond acquisition and comprehension into analysis, synthesis, evaluation, and application.

And, well, I've read about the increase in kids' television viewing time. I've heard about their inability to play games at recess: they just stand around, or maybe they play with a ready-made single-purpose toy for a bit and then they're bored. I'm told that kids, young people, don't go to the library anymore; they don't go to the used bookstores either, to trade in one handful of paperbacks for another. I know about the increase in learning disabilities. And I found out about grades inflation: Cs are now Bs, Bs are now As – 'So what do I give to students who really do get an A?' 'Trust me – you won't have that problem.' An exaggeration?

When I later taught courses at a university, basically applied philosophy – Informal Logic, Contemporary Moral Issues, Business Ethics – I discovered right away that essays on controversial issues were way over most of the students' heads. I soon started giving an open book reading comprehension quiz for each essay I assigned; it doubled as a guide to the main points of the essay. I couldn't teach them to assess what they didn't even understand.

And in three out of three courses, students told me that the kind of thinking I was demanding, essentially critical thinking, was a new way of thinking: they hadn't had to do it before. Arts majors, Science majors, and Business majors, even third and fourth year students – they all said the same thing.

And then – I happened to be in an Accounting class, watching students present case studies. The second group was very impressive. They sure had their act together. Respectfully in their suits and ties, standing at business attention, their voices projecting confidence, they introduced themselves as Wannick, Smith, and Pratsk: 'We thank you for choosing us as your Accounting consultants, and we are happy to present to you today our analysis ... ' They had rehearsed, that much was clear. And the power point presentation sure was slick: titles variously fonted with fade-ins and fade-outs, points neatly aligned and bulletted, graphics full of colour and icons – it looked just like the real thing. The class applauded.

I mumbled a query to the prof sitting next to me. 'Suitcoats and power point aside, which group had the better analysis?' 'The first group – these guys missed some important discrepancies in the accounts.' Hm. And if they didn't get an A, there was hope, I thought.

Then again, no there wasn't. The week after, the Student Union held an air band competition.

What do you want me to say?

Who among us has not heard the student in distress, claiming not to know 'what the professor wants'? As if getting good grades is dependent on finding out each professor's hidden idiosyncrasies – on figuring out how to please. This attitude has become very prevalent, and I've seen students paralysed by it. A professor will assign an essay, and students who are uncertain about how to proceed believe it's because they don't know what the professor wants; they truly believe they're missing some crucial bit of information. Of course, the real reason for their uncertainty is usually their poor academic skills – they don't know enough about the topic to generate some ideas or opinions with which they can then play around and organize into a paper. But instead of heading to the library or the Internet, they wander the halls and poll other students, trying to discover 'what the professor wants'.

My answer to this question – 'I want you to demonstrate your competence with the course content' – has been met with blank stares. If I'm lucky. Otherwise, it's been met with anger, as if I'm being maliciously evasive and unclear, as if I'm holding something back, as if I'm being unfair! I'll persist then: 'I want you to do exactly what I said – write a critical analysis of X' or 'Answer the four questions I pose' or whatever. 'Yeah, but, like, what do you mean? You aren't actually saying what you want us to do.' Students who are really keen to 'succeed' might come right out with it: 'But what do you want me to say? Tell me what to say and I'll say it!' I imagine the rest of the conversation. 'Well if I did that, I'd be writing your essay for you.' Responded to with 'Oh could you do that? That would be really helpful. And could I borrow your notes for your lecture? Oh and I missed the reading guide you handed out for the chapters we were to have read. And when will you be giving us the exam questions? And the answers? So we know what you want?'

(Thinking the problem might be lack of imagination as well as lack of knowledge, I've started giving students specific examples of what I want: for one course, I prepared four versions of a specific assignment, an A, a B, a C, and a D; when I work with students to help them improve their writing skills so they can pass our Writing Competency Test, I give them lots of examples of essays that would pass. But it takes an accomplished pianist to hear the difference between a Rubenstein performance and a Kiwanis Festival performance. It sounds the same to the person-next-door. I've learned that often the students who 'need' examples of good papers are exactly the students who can't see the difference anyway.)

It used to be that one was careful about image, careful to make it represent reality. You didn't want to give 'the wrong impression' – 'wrong' meaning one that was inaccurate, one that really wasn't you. Now people are careful to present the image of what they *want* to be. Or worse, if they are aiming to please, the image of what they think *the other wants* them to be.

Why is this attention to image so dangerous? There are two reasons. One, we are losing the ability to see through it. Quite simply, the ability to think is becoming obsolete. My students provide me with the evidence. When I first taught critical thinking, I took for granted that they would *understand* the material – the letters to the editor, the informal essays. My objective was to teach them to *critically assess* the material. Surprise! Indeed I was surprised – and appalled and enraged – to discover that they *couldn't* understand the material. And so teaching them to critically think about what they couldn't even understand was – well – difficult. (And these are university students, the cream of the crop, academically speaking.) Now if we can't understand the substance, let alone evaluate it, of course we'll be at the mercy of the pretence.

And this leads me to the second danger. A vicious circle will surely develop: if people can't respond to the substance anyway, why spend time on it, why *not* just focus on the pretence? But if we spend all our time cultivating the pretence, there will eventually be no substance. So it won't be 'image above all': it'll become 'image *is* all'! First you separate image from reality, then you focus exclusively on image, then you've got no reality, nothing's real anymore. Read William Gibson's *Idoru*.

So no wonder the students fret, 'Okay I get it, I have to have an introduction, a body, and a conclusion. But what do I put – I mean, what do you want me to put – in the paragraphs in the middle?' Hm. *Does it matter?*

Sexism and Teaching: The Elephant in the Room

Back in 1996, I was fortunate enough to get a job teaching a few courses at a university: several sections of a non-credit remedial English language course, a section of critical thinking, and various applied ethics courses. At the end of the second year, I was notified by the Dean that my student evaluations for the critical thinking course were too low, and I was asked to submit a self-assessment, along with an outline of proposed changes, were I allowed to teach the course the following year.

I submitted the following (slightly edited). (*Skip ahead at any time to the elephant in the room.*)

• • •

First, let me say that I was a bit surprised to receive [your] letter. One, I don't think scores of 3.3 and 3.25 on a scale of 5 are unacceptable; they're not what I would like, but they translate to a 'satisfactory' (to use the grading scheme we use for our students) 65%. Two, given the 'uprising' early in the year, to have brought the course and myself to the favourable side of neutral is, I think, admirable. ...

Regardless, you continue to have concerns about my teaching ability, so I will continue to try to alleviate those concerns. I'll start by describing changes made [following the uprising]:

1) I agreed, after an hour of consensus-reaching discussion with the class, to weight the 'crapbook' assignment (the first assignment which, I believe, started it all, for which students were to simply find examples of logically fallacious reasoning in the media and explain the fallacy) as low as 5% instead of 15%. The remaining 10% could be made up however each student wanted, in 5% chunks, choosing from the crapbook (so for those who did well, it could count the

15% it was originally supposed to count), an in-class test on the fallacies, a homework assignment schematizing the argument of one of the weekly assigned essays, and/or a participation mark.

2) I agreed to consider quantity alone for the participation mark (i.e., it didn't matter what the student said, as long as s/he opened her/his mouth …).

3) I reduced the length of the final exam (which was originally planned to be exactly like the mid-term, which, you may recall, was thought to be too long) by half for Parts A and B. (Part C, which required the student to argue a position on a given issue, was left as is.)

4) I re-calculated the mark for the mid-term as if Parts A and B had been half as long, with no maximum (i.e., if a student originally scored 23 out of 40, re-calculation gave the student 23 out of 20).

5) I used the mastery approach for the final essay assignment: that is, students could rewrite their essay an unlimited number of times, each time having it marked – thoroughly annotated by me and a number value assigned. Additionally, I scheduled individual student conferences to discuss my feedback, spending up to two hours per student (on top of my usual office hours). (I heard another faculty member say he simply didn't have the time to do that. I made the time. Pretty good, don't you think, for a sessional instructor who gets paid half as much per course as a Lecturer gets paid, never mind what a Professor gets paid …)

6) I also added an extra class each week, attendance optional, an hour in length, during which 'practice Parts A and B' were worked through. (Way beyond the call of duty here …)

7) I made a public apology in class to anyone I may have

offended or ridiculed. (I wish you could have seen the expressions of many as I did so – it was clear they thought the accusations were a 'crock of shit'.) (Also, I would still like to know, by the way, exactly what the basis was for the accusations of rudeness and disrespect – it's been really difficult to stop doing whatever it is that's perceived as rude and disrespectful when I don't know what it is.) (One student said I didn't ridicule, I 'teased' – I do think this is much more accurate; one teases good-naturedly, not maliciously.)

With all of these changes, the average of the class was, as you requested, not below 69. It was, in fact, 69.5 (excluding, of course, three students who didn't write the exam and/or the major essay).

Now, as for your requested "self-assessment and an outline of what [I] might propose to change next year" – it was decided, was it not, half way through the first term, that I would not be allowed to teach [the critical thinking course] next year? Nevertheless, I have carefully considered each criterion, and my score (in parentheses, below), and submit the following responses.

Course Presentation

1. Required texts were useful (3.50) – I examined 14 texts before choosing the two I used. I chose a logical reasoning text that was fairly easy (I anticipated *not* having a class full of Philosophy majors) and rather entertaining (there were cartoons throughout). I also chose an argument reader – an anthology of essays on topics as diverse as capital punishment, abortion, smoking, war, mowing one's lawn, sexism, civil rights, aboriginal rights, and the value of a university education; the essays were varied in length (about 3 to 15 pages) and difficulty (newspaper article to academic

essay). *Without further feedback, I'm not sure what change to make here ...*

2. Other instructional material (3.82) – I'm not sure whether quality or quantity was evaluated: in addition to the texts, I used a few handouts as supplements; I also prepared a quiz on overheads to summarize, review, and measure learning outcome achievement at the end of each chapter. Should I have used more materials? Perhaps the overheads were not easily seen by those in the back? *Again, I'm not sure what change is in order here.*

3. Assignments/Papers useful (2.94) – First of all, because I extended the deadline for the major essay four times (if I hadn't, there would have been a lot more than three students who received a zero), these evaluations were done *before* the major essay was done. This is important: I believe that many students experienced *significant* benefits from the mastery approach and the intensive one-on-one appointments with me. Half of the students eventually wrote an A essay; the average was 78%; they did learn; it was useful.

This score was based, then, on two assignments: the crapbook and the argument schema assignment (which was optional). I can't believe the crapbook assignment wasn't useful: as mentioned above, students were to find examples of logically fallacious reasoning on television, in the newspaper, on the radio, in videos, in political party material, etc. And as for the argument schema, being able to read an essay and extract the argument (the author's point and his/her reasons for claiming that point) should be considered useful to anyone who considers the course useful. (Perhaps that's the problem. See item 8.) *So, again, I'm not sure what change is in order here.*

However, knowing now how valuable the mastery approach to the major essay was, I'd use the approach on a smaller essay (a mini version of what the major essay would be) during the first term – and then perhaps not use it with the major essay.

4. Tests (3.39) – I'm not sure what the question was (unfortunately I have only my score sheet, not the questionnaire originals), but I don't see any problem at all with the one test: students had to identify and explain the fallacy present in three of five given items, and they had the entire class (80 minutes) in which to do this. Perhaps students wanted more tests? They could have said so when we discussed the grading scheme at the beginning of the course. Perhaps they didn't think the test was fair? Only 12 of them opted to write it (recall, it was optional) and the average was 73%. *Again, what to change?*

5. Labs/Seminars – N/A

6. Appropriate difficulty (3.00) – While a few students clearly said that the course was a much needed refreshing challenge, 12 of 18 students noted that the course was too difficult. I disagree. And in a way, that's all there is to it. I think I'm in a better position to know what a second year Philosophy/Critical Thinking course should be like than my students (at least, I'd better be!).

I'd like to point out that 'appropriate difficulty' is a problem for most professors here at [name removed] University (it received the second lowest score) – I am assuming the problem is that the courses are perceived to be 'too difficult', not 'not difficult enough'.

The texts I chose were specifically written for this kind of course, at this level, and so they should not have been too difficult. In fact, the logical reasoning text I chose was easier than the one [the department chair] had been using.

I think a large part of the problem was students' reading skills. The argument reader was, quite simply, way over their heads. Many of them even had difficulty with the newspaper articles (which are typically written at a grade eight reading level) – difficulty even with *comprehension*: they couldn't tell me what the point was, let alone what the reasons for that point were. And this ability is prerequisite to the course, which focused on *evaluation*: whether or not the reasons were *good* reasons. That Part B on both the midterm and final exam ("Read the passage below, then explain and evaluate the argument.") was the most poorly done supports my analysis. [A colleague's] passing comment about the Nelson-Denny results at [name removed] University (there was an alarming number of students who tested at a grade four reading level) also supports my analysis. The course I'm currently teaching also supports my analysis: at the beginning of the class, I give an open book quiz on the assigned reading, and questions like "Does Berns support capital punishment" are not always correctly answered; that is to say, it's not unusual for students to have read a whole essay on capital punishment and not know whether the author was supporting it or attacking it.

One could say 'teach to the lowest common denominator' – but if we're always teaching to the sparrows, when do the bluebirds get their education? Surely, university is *for* the bluebirds. Or one could say 'start at where the students are' – but this is not high school; students are not required by law to be in my classroom; if the course is too difficult, then they shouldn't take it (or, at least, not expect an A grade).

And yet, and yet ... Perhaps next time, I'll spend the first month on reading comprehension: I'll start by having the students read just a one-paragraph piece and tell me what the issue is; once they can do that, I'll see if they can tell me what the point is; after a week or so, we'd graduate to a letter to the editor; then a short article; then I'll have them tell me the point as well as the reasons; and maybe by second term, we'll get to academic essays. But that would be a Remedial Reading course, not a Critical Thinking course.

Another large part of the problem is student effort. Attendance was low, or at least lower than I expected (I know, you'll say this is my fault), and many students seldom put in the three hours it took to be prepared (most had just read the essay – they were also supposed to have figured out the point and the reasons for that point, and thought about relevance, adequacy, and truth, the criteria for a good argument). Had they done this every week, had they put in this practice, I maintain the exams wouldn't have seemed so difficult. More than one student supported the idea of graded quizzes based on the readings; they were too busy doing the homework for other courses, they said, which was marked. In the same vein, another suggested giving marks for attendance. Frankly, I find this really pathetic: if students need to be rewarded by marks to do the homework, and even to attend the class, then they aren't really interested; and if that's the case, again, why are they taking the course? I don't want to encourage such 'marks dependency' nor do I think I should have to entice, coax, cajole, or bribe students – at the university level. However, if most of the other professors here at [name removed] University *do* give marks for attendance and homework completion, then I can understand why the students were less motivated in my class. *And so, much against my better judgement, I am giving quizzes on the readings in my current course; I've made them 'open book' quizzes and have designed them to act as 'advance organizers' for our discussion and review notes for examination preparation, so perhaps it's not turning out too badly; I would consider continuing with this practice.*

And part of the problem was writing skills. Some (many?) students resented the fact that I 'marked for grammar and stuff' ... ; one specifically said on the comment sheet of her evaluation that it was unfair of me to have marked the writing. Am I not to consider the quality of writing when I grade essays?

What other changes would I make? To be honest, I'd do a little of the Remedial Reading suggested above. But you have often told us not to lower our standards. You've also said make sure they get Bs. You can't have it both ways. (Unless incoming students are better prepared or become better prepared very quickly.)

8. Course Content Valuable (3.12) – Well, this is a sad comment on our society, isn't it. The ability to think clearly and critically is not valuable. Or perhaps the students think they already know how to think clearly and critically. I think that's more likely. Trying to get through the 'It's my opinion and everyone's entitled to their opinion' attitude was like trying to walk underwater. *Perhaps next time I'll open with a video of "The Jerry Springer Show" and then follow it with a video of "Studio 2" – to try to get them to see that they do have something to learn ... Though if I start the course by telling them what they can't do, I'll be perceived even more as insulting them.*

(Reminder that you can jump ahead to the elephant in the room if you've had enough.)

Instructor

9. Course Objectives were Clear (3.56) – I articulated them orally and wrote them on the board at least four times throughout the year: "To succeed in this course, whether you're reading, writing, listening, or speaking, you have to know (i) what the point is, (ii) what the reasons are for that

point, and (iii) whether or not the reasons are good ones – considering relevance, adequacy, and truth." And every Thursday, when we considered that week's essay, these questions were asked, repeatedly. In fact, even the first class icebreaker introduced them to the fundamental concept of the course: they were to introduce themselves to someone by saying 'Hi, my name is X and I believe A because B'. *How many times am I expected to convey course objectives? How could I have been more clear?*

10. Grading, Evaluation Criteria (3.22) – Assuming this addressed whether or not the criteria were clear, I confess bafflement. I must have said their writing had to be "clear and correct" a hundred times. I put students' crapbook items (voluntarily submitted items that received diverse marks) on the opaque projector so students could see what a 5/5 was like and compare it to a 1/5, and I walked them through: 'See, here the student has stated clearly what fallacy is present, that's one mark; then the student has defined the fallacy, there's the second mark, etc.' When I handed back the mid-term exam, I included perfect answers to every one of the fallacy items, and I had written out an 'A' answer to Part B and included that as well. *What more to do?*

11. Consistent, Fair Grading (2.56) – Almost my lowest score. Amazing, given that I marked blind (that is, students identified their work by student number only) in order to eliminate bias; I also, of course, marked all Part As, then went back and marked all Part Bs, and so on, to further ensure consistency; and, also of course, I marked recursively – that is, part way through, I looked again at the first few answers to be sure I hadn't drifted, and I looked again at the middle few when I was at the end; lastly, neither [the department chair nor the only other Philosophy professor] thought my marking was inconsistent when I offered a

sample for their examination. *Suggestions for change?*
12. Helpful Comments and Feedback (3.00) – Again, I remind you that this was *before* the major essay assignment. Nevertheless, this is again a puzzle. Perhaps the students couldn't recognize the help; perhaps they thought that my Socratic questions leading them to the light were just bludgeoning them into the dirt. Or perhaps they just *wouldn't* recognize my help. More on this later.
13. Meaningful examples (3.56) – What do you want me to say about this one? I do try and *will continue to try* to provide meaningful examples.
14. Organized, well-planned (3.33) – Again, a mystery. I am *compulsively* organized. I recall twice forgetting to assign homework questions, and once I put the wrong overhead on the screen. Is that really, seriously, a problem? *There is, simply, no need for change here.*
15. Opportunity for Questions (3.72) – I consistently solicit questions in class; I am in my office during office hours. *No room for improvement here.*
16. Clear, Effective Answers (3.11) – This was the first time I taught this course and so I was fielding questions in this area for the first time. Yes, there were times I was not as incisive as I might have been. *I'll do better next time.*
17. Encouraged independent thinking (3.44) – [see below]
18. Challenged, provoked thought (3.50) – [see below]

    On both criteria, more mystery. Rather, misunderstanding. I would've thought both of these items would have scored over 4.0. It makes me think that these students have never been exposed to the Socratic pedagogical style before. And actually, I do think this is part of the problem. If most professors lecture, then indeed I am unusual, indeed students don't know how to take my constant questions, my constant challenges – perhaps they take them as insults. Perhaps when I present an opposing view, they think I'm genuinely disagreeing with them and they are offended. Perhaps when I insist on reasons, they think I'm insisting that they're wrong (and that I'm right – and hence I'm not encouraging independent thinking but, instead, I'm encouraging them to agree with me ...).

Also, we're back to 'It's my opinion and I'm entitled to it' and a built-in difficulty with this kind of course: not only do I push (and I do – I push, I prod, I prick), I do so close to their hearts – the content (abortion, capital punishment, the pursuit of profit ...) is more personal than, say, physics.

Next time, I'd do a lot of advance explanation of my pedagogical style. The Rasool text has an excellent 'Note to the Student' explaining that when professors ask for reasons, they are not insulting you ... apparently I'm not the first Critical Thinking professor to have been so misunderstood ... I really didn't think I had to explain all of this ...
19. Made the course interesting (2.78) – Wow. If issues such as those in the argument reader (see above) and assignments like the crapbook (see above) aren't interesting, I don't know what is. (Actually, if they aren't, then the student should've dropped the course.) One of our classes was a United Nations simulation in which students were Iraq and Israel, Somalia and Bosnia, and Ireland, and the rest of us were whatever country we wanted to be. In another class, we played a game I made up called 'Argument Chess.'

I speak with an animated and enthusiastic voice (which also happens to be genuine). While I can't move around the room, I do move back and forth at the front rather than planting myself in one spot for the whole class. I vary the mode of presentation (Tuesdays was mostly text and oral with overheads; Thursdays was mostly text and visual and then discussion – in twos, small groups, and large groups, sometimes assigned groupings, sometimes student-selected).

I think I made the course as interesting as I need to; I am not wholly responsible for whether or not the students are interested.

Honestly, I think there was something else going on here ... *The elephant in the room.*

20. Clear effective voice (4.06) – Can I assume this score is acceptable?

21. Responsive out-of-class (3.82) – How would they know? 90% of my office hours were not used. (And again, this was before the intensive appointments about their essays.) *No improvement needed here.*

22. Up-to-date knowledge (3.50) – I confess, I do not have up-to-date knowledge on all the issues we discussed. But I don't think I am expected to: when we evaluate argument, we say 'If the premises are true, this would be a valid/sound argument' – we leave the determination of truth to those qualified.

23. Learning Environment (2.44) – Surely who's in the class affects the learning environment as much as, if not more than, the professor. I must confess I think the critical thinking course was a case of 'a few bad apples' – I agree with the student who said, on the comment sheet, "There were a lot of immature students in this class who didn't respect [the prof] and gave her a hard time no matter what she did."

You may ask then, why was this so? Why did they give me such a hard time? Good question. One student suggested that it was because I didn't have a Ph.D. Though a few others complained that I constantly flaunted my degrees! (Like I'd flaunt an M.A.)

Another suggested that things would've been different had I been teaching in the auditorium rather than in a portable.

Apparently being in the portables is a low-status indicator.

Another suggested that students were so free to express their opinion in my class, they kind of got carried away.

A few said that I shouldn't have let them get away with so much, I should have asserted my authority more; and others complained that the class was run like a dictatorship.

One complained that I was always right and the student was always wrong and I made that perfectly clear. (If I say the answer's 5.4 and my student says it's 3.2, I'd better be the one who's right, and I'd better make it clear to the student!)

What do I think? How do I explain the hostility?

1) I think a lot had to do with the marks – as I pointed out earlier, the uprising occurred only after the first assignment was marked. Perhaps some of the hostility toward me was displaced anger and frustration with their grade. *Next time then, the first assignment will be earlier, and while it will be marked, it won't count. Also, I'd like to say that next time, the exam will be worth 30% and everything else will be weighted according to each student's preference, decisions to be made at the end of the course. Perhaps also next time I should find out before the course begins what the average grade is supposed to be.*

2) Also, my style is somewhat personal. I would often share bits of what I was doing or had done, as conscious role modelling; I'd say things like 'That's exactly an issue I'm struggling with right now in a paper I'm working on' or I'd refer to my own article on euthanasia when we read the anthology selection on euthanasia. Unfortunately student comments indicate that this was perceived as bragging – *so I guess I won't do this next time.*

3) My guess is that some students simply didn't take the course seriously right from the beginning because (a) they thought that Philosophy was an easy, rather than a rigorous,

discipline; (b) they thought that any course without a prerequisite would be a breeze; (c) they were convinced they already knew how to think; (d) they assumed that since the course was very much about opinions, it would be easy because, after all, 'everyone's entitled to their own opinion' so all that's necessary is to *have* an opinion ... .
4) Unlike other courses, there is very little content in a critical thinking course to 'save' them; there is no research to be done, there is no knowledge per se to acquire – this is pure critical thinking (the stuff that brings their other marks down) (here it is the *only* stuff). I find it interesting that with blind marking, the top student was a Math student; there is a close relation between Math and Philosophy in their disciplined clarity of thought; Math is right up there with Physics and Philosophy regarding GRE scores.) One of my [former] professors recently said to me that she first thought this course would be easy to teach because there's no content; then she realized it was the hardest to teach – because there's no content. And since it's purely a skill course, practice is essential – and I don't think most students did the practice I assigned. Perhaps like Statistics, this is a course that students need to take twice to pass.

• • •

Of course, even while I was preparing the above response, it occurred to me that all of it could be irrelevant, an exhaustive and exhausting bucket of red herrings. Why did the students complain? Why were they so resistant to my questions, my comments, my instruction? *Because I'm female. That's the elephant in the room.* There's no way men (and many of my students were male) are going to take instruction from a woman. There's no way men are going to concede to a woman, grant that she's right and they're wrong. There's no way men are going to consider women competent. [I found out later, regarding another course I was teaching, that a male student actually organized a meeting to prepare a list of complaints about me, one of which was "She puts comments on our essays." Seriously.]

But I came of age in the 70s, obtained my teaching degree and my first teaching position in the early 80s, when we were developing non-sexist language and revamping the dead-white-male canon, and taught joyously and enthusiastically through the 80s; I then moved to a backwoods sort of place that I thought was just behind the times a bit – through the 90s, I assumed the rest of the world was progressing in the direction set in the 70s and 80s.

So one, I thought that my sex couldn't be the explanation for my experience at the university, or at least not the whole explanation, because we were so past sexism. And two, I thought that that explanation was so obvious as to not merit mention; I assumed everyone my age or younger was as up-to-speed as I was about sexism in the classroom.

I didn't know about the backlash. I didn't realize that all the ground we had gained, and then some, had been lost. So I was wrong. So very wrong. On both points.

Some time after I'd prepared my detailed, anguished response to the Dean's letter, I happened to stand outside a male colleague's class for a few minutes (I'd been invited to do a special talk on ethics and economics), and I was amazed at the quiet: no one was interrupting him; no one was challenging his every word; no one was competing with him. That is to say, they were not trying to undermine his authority; they had accepted it. *Because he was male.*

Just in case you haven't had enough, before I was completely 'fired' (a.k.a. not asked to teach any other courses), yet another (male) student went to the Dean to complain. I may be wrong, but I suspect that he never would have done so if a *male* professor had refused, given the circumstances indicated in my response below, to increase his grade. The following is the response I prepared to *that* complaint.

• • •

Please consider this as comment/rebuttal to Cody's allegation of unfair treatment in [Ethics for Social Science]:

1. I don't fully understand Cody's first point: "with a considerable amount of commentary and another re-write, [his first paper] was worth at least a pass." Students were not allowed to submit re-writes of the first paper (not one, and certainly not "another"), and any "commentary" he wanted to include in his paper would have been, should have been, included in the version he submitted.

Also, I'd like to point out that I met with every student, Cody included, on a one-to-one basis, to discuss in detail their first paper – partly because it was indeed their first, partly because the final exam would be similar, and partly because such feedback is simply excellent pedagogy and my classes are usually small enough that I can do this.

2. I did not grant an extension to any student for the second paper (as Cody claims) – certainly not to a student who "simply forgot about the due date." I did allow a student to hand in the *third* assignment a week after it was due: I had changed the due date, moving it earlier by a week, and she apparently was not present when I announced the change (she was working to the original due date as per the course outline). Also, I did allow two students to resubmit their second paper, but this was clearly not permission to rewrite: while both students had identified the secondary source they used, they did not include quotation marks wherever they quoted – I merely refused to mark their papers until they inserted the quotation marks (so I could clearly see what was their work and what was not). Believing that Cody, and perhaps others, misunderstood that as permission to rewrite (and therefore evidence in unfairness), I explained at some

length to the class as a whole exactly what I was permitting those two students to do; unfortunately, that was a day Cody arrived late, and I had to therefore repeat the explanation – it's possible my repeat explanation was abbreviated, leaving Cody without full understanding the distinction between 'rewrite' and 'resubmit'.

Further, I'd like to point out that with regard to the second paper, students were required to submit an extensive outline four weeks before it was due. I provided extensive feedback two weeks hence (again, meeting with students individually), leaving them two weeks to rework (if necessary) and write up the paper – I, thus, 'built in' the re-write option. Cody, however, did not take advantage of this: he did not submit an outline, but, instead, simply submitted a completed paper on the final due date. (Such preliminary feedback was also allowed for the third assignment; again, Cody did not take advantage of that.)

Further still, with regard to the second paper, I did allow a few students to re-write their paper correcting their grammar and punctuation (but not changing the content at all); they could then resubmit it for a slight increase in the grade (for example, a C+ would turn into a B-). Cody was one of these few students, but he did not bother to correct and resubmit his paper.

3. With regard to Cody's class participation mark, those marks were based not only on quantity, but also on quality of contribution. As for quantity, attendance was also taken into account: Cody missed at least two full classes, which I consider substantial in a course totalling a mere twelve classes. As for quality, Cody's contributions were very poor. For example, in a discussion about whether one is morally 'allowed' (the weak version) or morally 'obligated' (the strong version) to tell someone that someone else is HIV

positive, Cody's contribution was something like 'And what about at places like Casino Rama where they have a separate trash can for needles in the washrooms?' Given that that discussion occurred during the *last* class, such a comment is indicative of Cody's persisting inability to understand and follow the arguments that comprise the course content; that, not my unfairness, explains his failing grade.

It is certainly quite possible that I use different assessment standards than Cody is used to: ethics is quite a different course than, say, marketing or accounting. However, I believe I use standards appropriate for the course, and they are, thus, not unfair. And I have used the same standards for Cody as I have used for the other students in that course – which is to say, again, that I have not been unfair. (Of course, much depends on one's definition of 'fair' – as this was a topic we explored at some length in the course, it's disappointing, but not surprising, to see Cody using the term with such imprecision.)

• • •

As I say, if I were a male professor, I doubt Cody would have gone to the Dean.

Perhaps more importantly, *if I were a male professor*, I probably would have responded to the Dean's request for a response to the evaluations with just a short paragraph full of generalities about possible changes.

And that would have been the end of it.

Visionary

When I read about Nipissing University's Students in Free Enterprise (NUSIFE), which is a group of students who undertake projects "intended to increase the public's awareness of entrepreneurship and business-related subjects," it occurred to me to wonder why such an endeavour is undertaken only by business students.

Consider the projects listed below – then imagine …
- "Global Crusaders" educated high school students about minimum wages and exchange rates in five different countries – why not educate them about gender issues in five different countries …
- "Team Builders" led team-building exercises during a weekend program at the YMCA – my guess is that sociology students' take on team-building would be quite different than that of business students …
- "Junior Tycoons" were high school students who presented a basic business plan – why not have "Junior Diplomats" present a recess plan based on insights from political science, history, and psychology …
- "Budgeting for Mental Health Patients" – how about "Philosophy for Mental Health Patients" …
- "My First Bank Account" – whatever happened to "My First Library Card" …
- "Nipissing East Community Opportunities" received a marketing plan – they could have used an environmental assessment plan …
- "Show Me the Money" was about financial planning guidelines on the web – how about "Show Me the Stars", about astronomy on the web …
- "A Feasibility Study" was presented to graphic arts

students – how about presenting them with an ethics study …

Such projects, both by training students to apply their knowledge outside academia and by increasing the visibility of business in the outside world, probably contribute to the stranglehold business – business activities and business interests – has on the world; therefore, suggesting that similar endeavours be undertaken by humanities and science students as well is more than an exercise in imagination – it's an identification of responsibility.

This particular infiltration of business is so developed that there are actually *competitions* among universities for their SIFE teams. Yes, there are poetry and drama competitions too, but poems and plays don't reach out and engage the community in the same way; they just present to, perform for, the community (except for those cool workplace theatre guerrilla groups). Perhaps science does a little better; there are, of course, the annual science fairs, but from time to time I also see students out in the field with their lab kits.

This lack of engagement is rampant throughout the humanities curriculum. We teach our English students how to appreciate and write poetry, but not how to find a literary agent; how to appreciate and write drama, but not how to produce a play. Philosophy students are great at clarifying concepts and values, identifying hidden assumptions, testing for consistency and coherence; psychology students know all about how our minds and emotions work; sociology students know about people in groups, small and large, in cultures and subcultures and countercultures; history students know what hasn't worked. Along with our students of gender studies and native studies and our other social science students, humanities students (the humanities focus on humanity – and who, what, are we talking about when all is said and done?), and of course our science students (what is humanity but one bunch of carbon-based organisms among many), would be great consultants – if they had any consulting skills. But we don't teach them how to write a proposal, how to contract for business, or how to manage a project.

Until we do these things, our humanities and science students will be dependent on business students as go-betweens and as enablers. And since business students, by definition apparently, have profit as their motivator, their purpose, and their goal, there is bound to be a certain amount of unfulfilled potential. Business students are not likely to set up Sociologists, Inc. or History Is Us. Nor are they even likely to engage the services of non-business students as consultants.

OPAS (the Office for Partnerships for Advanced Skills) is another example of the deficiency I'm trying to expose. It's a partnership between Ontario universities and Canadian companies with a mandate to "foster more effective relations between universities and companies who hire and maintain a highly skilled workforce" and "respond to requests and develop initiatives that promote increased use of university-based resources including advanced skills development." One might be forgiven, therefore, for thinking it was pretty inclusive. This seems indicated even by the Special Events & Programs (which include a Visionary Seminar Series, Industry Sector Symposia, Internship & Reciprocal Exchange Programs and the development of a National Network) and by the Skills Development statement (which says "In knowledge industries, skills requirements advance and change, creating new needs [and] OPAS responds to these changing skills needs with solutions designed and delivered by leading university programs across Ontario").

However, a close look reveals that there isn't a whole lot of room for humanities and social science; there's something for science and engineering (an auto parts symposium is listed, as well as a biotech sector symposium), but it seems that the university programs they're talking about partnering with are pretty much the B.B.A. and M.B.A. Their website welcome page confirms this: "In today's knowledge-based economy, business organizations are faced with the need to address constant changes in operating practices, human capital requirements, and technology." That page is pure business buzz ("human *capital*"?!). (And there you do see the specification – "*business* organizations … .")

Indeed, had I visited the OPAS website first, I wouldn't have been so surprised to discover that the keynote speaker (the only speaker) at the "Visionary 2000" seminar was the CEO of the Royal Bank (how much more focussed on business, profit, money, can you get?). And the very fact that his talk, nothing more than a Royal Bank promo, was billed as *visionary* indicates just how much we need to correct this deficiency.

Useless Humanities

That a humanities degree is useless for the workforce says more about our workforce than the degree. It says that we value, that we'll pay for, someone to provide cars, electric toothbrushes, and running shoes. But not beauty and insight.

It doesn't have to be that way. Imagine a world in which companies had, along with finance departments to look after their money and maintenance departments to keep things clean, art departments to make the place beautiful. Municipalities could have art departments too, right alongside their legal departments and transit departments, to keep the city beautiful. Or entertaining. Or edifying. Depending on your view of the role of art.

Provinces could have, in addition to the Ministries of Environment, Energy, and Revenue, a Ministry of Music. Yes, of course, there is a Ministry of Culture and Recreation, and that's close. And there are provincial arts councils. Close again. But they're just administrative bodies: there are no practicing artists on staff whose job it is to *do* their art. (The Ministry of Environment, on the other hand, has, for example, biologists on staff whose job it is to do biology.)

We'd have municipal and provincial concert halls and theatres and galleries with full complements of staff – that is, full-time paid musicians, playwrights, actors, painters, providing a year-round schedule of daily events. Attendance would be covered by our taxes, just as is our use of the roads.

Imagine a world in which video stores had as many videos of dance performances as of war movies. A world in which poets and short story writers and novelists read in movie theatres. And people paid to get in. As many people. Hell, our lit grads might make a living!

Imagine a world in which we valued knowledge about ourselves as much as knowledge about our money. And we paid philosophers, psychologists, and sociologists as much as we pay financial advisors.

Imagine a PR department hiring a historian to manage the information, to develop true, coherent archives. With intelligent analysis.

We have concert halls, libraries, and museums. We have jobs for musicians, poets, and historians. But we have so many more banks and stores and restaurants. We thus have so many more jobs for business majors (the managers and the accountants) and non-majors (the clerks and waiters), for people whose raison d'être is to make or serve profit – not beauty, joy, insight, or understanding.

Is it truly supply and demand? Do we really have the world we want to have? Yes and no. If we asked the philosophers and psychologists and sociologists, we'd know that we want what we're used to, so supply creates demand as much as, if not more than, demand creates supply. And we'd know that pressure can modify our wants: customs and marketing strategies can compromise our autonomy if we don't pay attention. To our real desires, our real goals. To our joys, to our hopes. (Every now and then, I think things may be different in Europe. But how would I know – it's not the sort of thing that the U.S. or even Canada puts on the news. Around and around …)

And anyway, so what? So what if a humanities degree is useless in the workforce. Not all value need be tangled up with the economy, with business, with the workplace. (Have you mistaken your job for your life?) Not everything has to have a price. Not everything need be, or *can* be, sold. Or bought. Some things just are. (The recognition and appreciation of beauty and joy. The cultivation of curiosity and interest. The achievement of exhilaration and understanding … .)

Dismissing Philosophy and Philosophers / Philosophy – Misunderstood

"Yes, well, that's a philosophical question, isn't it." So, what, the question's unimportant? Because it can't be answered with quantitative certainty? But philosophical questions *can* be answered with more or less strength, more or less adequacy. Read on.

Also, since there's no absolutely right or wrong answer to most philosophical questions, the consensus seems to be that anyone can 'do' philosophy. In one sense, that's true. Anyone can do philosophy. Anyone can do physics too. It's just that incompetence, inadequacy, will be more apparent in the latter case. Because there are right and wrong answers. Most of the time. At least at the lower levels.

But one can make mistakes in when engaging in philosophical reasoning too. It's just that we haven't trained people to see mistakes in reasoning as much as we've trained them to see mistakes in arithmetic. (Which is, partly, why people mistakenly think all opinions are equally valid.)

Not only are philosophical questions dismissed, philosophers too are dismissed. After all, they're no better than the rest of us. Their opinions are no more valid. I'm starting to see the dismissal of scientists in the same way: it occurs when the person doesn't understand science – after all, if you don't understand the scientific process of hypothesis formulation and testing, if you don't understand how scientists arrive at their opinions, you won't consider scientific opinions any more valid. Similarly with philosophers: if you don't understand the relationship of premise and conclusion, the necessity of relevance ...

That it took so long for philosophy to become a high school course suggests that most people misunderstand philosophy (and philosophers). Even within academia, however, there seems to be confusion. Two PhDs expressed surprise at the title of my masters' thesis in Philosophy ("The Issue of Consent in Sex and Sexual Assault"); both seemed to think that philosophy was stuff like 'If a tree falls and no one's there, does it make a sound?' or 'Does the table really exist?' Philosophy *is* that. But not, at all, only that.

Metaphysics (Is the table real?) and epistemology (What's the difference between believing something and knowing something?) are both areas of philosophy. So are ethics (How could/should we determine right and wrong?) and aesthetics (What do we mean when we say 'X is beautiful'?).

But so are social philosophy (Why is there war? Are affirmative action programs fair?), political philosophy (Which is better – liberalism or socialism? What is the nature of the just society?), and philosophical psychology or philosophy of mind (What is the relation between the mind and the brain?). And some areas have fields pretty large in themselves: environmental ethics (Should we use animals for experimentation? Do trees have rights?); business ethics (Is profit an acceptable motive? How do we define, exactly, a conflict of interest?); biomedical ethics (Is it right to pay someone for their organ donation? Is euthanasia immoral?).

Truth is philosophy is not so much a subject as a skill: philosophy is disciplined reflection. So there is, there can be, a 'philosophy of' anything or an 'anything philosophy': philosophy of science, philosophy of language, philosophy of education, philosophy of love, feminist philosophy, legal philosophy, etc. *Whenever you're examining the conceptual foundations*, especially for clarity or consistency, *you're doing philosophy*. Far from being the least relevant endeavour, philosophy is the most relevant: other disciplines deal with who, what, when, where, and how; philosophy deals mostly with why (after dealing with 'What exactly do you mean?').

One of the most misunderstood courses in university is a second year philosophy course called, variously, Critical Thinking, Clear Thinking, or Informal Logic. The template in such courses is 'I think X because Y'. The purpose of the course is to teach people to have reasons for their opinions – to have *good* reasons. Most of us know that something can't be *A* and *not-A* at the same time. But there are other rules of reason, rules we constantly break – and this constantly gets us into trouble. (Is your argument sound? Are your premises true? Are they valid – relevant and adequate?) What the course does is teach these rules of reason, the skills of thinking: it develops the capacity to analyze an issue, to break it down into its parts; to draw distinctions, identify assumptions, clarify concepts, understand connections; it trains one to check for coherence, consistency, and completeness. A philosophical analysis is a very careful examination and assessment.

A supervisor once said of me, after I had provided feedback on a sexual harassment brochure, 'I wish I had a mind like that'. It's a mind developed by the rigours of philosophy. It's a mind developed to be clear, to be precise, to be thorough. It's a disciplined mind. I may not tell you the answers. But by the time a philosopher's through, you'll know what all the important questions are (as well as how they're connected). You'll also have a pretty good idea of the *possible* answers, each with their implications.

Whether or not to quit your job, whether or not to have an abortion, whether or not to kill yourself – these are all philosophical questions. Even trying to determine why you feel depressed involves philosophical skills – to uncover and clarify perceptions, assumptions, expectations. In fact, while here in Canada and the U.S. when we advise someone to get counselling or therapy, we mean *psychological* counselling, there is also such a thing as *philosophical* counselling. It's a well developed field in Europe: it has its own journals, its different schools of thought; one can become a certified philosophical counsellor and hang out a shingle for business, much like the familiar psychological counsellor here. As a parallel to psychoanalysis, it makes perfect sense. After all, philosophy *is* analysis.

How Many Specialists Does It Take To Change A Lightbulb?

Every now and then, there is a swing in academia toward the holistic approach, toward systems theory, if you will. In this anti-atomistic, anti-reductionist view, the essence is the process, not the structure; what's important is not so much the thing, but the relationship between the thing and other things. I think of Fritjof Capra's work of fifteen years ago, *The Turning Point*, and I wonder if perhaps quantum physics will provide the necessary weight once and for all for critical mass so the pendulum will stop, making the atomistic view a thing of the past, permanently.

Given this, this need for seeing the relationships, not just the things, it's too bad people think 'jack of all, master of none'; it's too bad generalist degrees (the Bachelor of Liberal Arts, the Bachelor of Liberal Sciences) are considered almost worthless, while the only ones that seem to 'count' are the specialist degrees (a B.A. or a B.Sc. with a concentration in Some One Thing) – and the more specialist, the better (a Ph.D. in Some One Thing). On the contrary, the value should be on *generalist* degrees, more specifically, on *interdisciplinary* degrees, for only interdisciplinary studies focus on the relationships between, the interdependence of, things.

One reason, perhaps, for reluctance to make this paradigm shift is that 'dependence', as in 'the inter*dependence* of things', has a bad name – it's thought to be weak. Especially by men. Who rule the world. I think that's why communitarianism, with its emphasis on connectedness, isn't exactly usurping Rawls and company (including grandfather Kant). The concept of gestalt provides one way around this: the sum can be greater than its parts. Linguistics provides another: let's call it 'interactive' rather than 'interdependent'.

Of course part of the reason for the evolution of specialization is the quantity of information: one simply *can't* stay at the cutting edge in more than one area. This is true, but if everyone's at their own section of the edge, who's supervising the cutting? Are we going to allow our pattern to be one of chance? We need multi/interdisciplinary people, meta-people, to help put the pieces together. Philosophers, trained to examine conceptual foundations, are especially suited for this task; the plethora of 'philosophy of X' courses supports this. A philosophy of science course, for example, deals with the basis (not the basics) of science.

And I wonder if the drive to specialization hasn't become self-defeating. Knowledge is not power; it's knowing what to do with knowledge that's important; and it's knowing what knowledge you want or need that's important. I am repeatedly surprised to discover just how much of how many university courses never get past the knowledge/comprehension level, to use Bloom's taxonomy. They can't – because there's so much knowledge (if one is to specialize) to cover. True, many (mostly the Sciences) also get into application; and some (usually the Humanities) venture into interpretation and evaluation; but very few (almost Philosophy alone) has as its *focus* analysis and synthesis.

The value of a generalist approach, specifically of an interdisciplinary approach, is not just that it's appropriate to the nature of *things* – it's appropriate to the nature of the things' *problems*. Problems don't respect disciplinary boundaries; rather they go outside the lines, they leak from one field (supposing they even start in one field) into another and often still another, making the colours run together and leaving a trail of grey areas.

Solutions seem to depend then on an interdisciplinary approach. Economic solutions often fail because they haven't accounted for the psychology of the involved people;

environmental solutions fail when they don't recognize and incorporate the politics involved; social solutions can fail simply because the architecture, the design of the society's city, wasn't taken into account. The list goes on.

So who are you going to call? Specialist-busters: interdisciplinary generalists.

(Either that or an interdisciplinary committee of specialists, with no egos and excellent communication skills – one that *can change* the damn light bulb.)

Religion: Superstition and Habit
(a very brief primer)

I find it amazing that so many people still believe in God. I can only conclude that, in most cases, they just haven't thought about it. Because thinking about religion is the surest way to atheism. (Which is probably why so many religions discourage thought: come to God as a child [1] – whose intellectual faculties are quite insufficient for the task; trust in me, listen to me, I speak for God – you don't need to worry your little head about it.)

There are several classic arguments for the existence of God. But as Bertrand Russell (*Why I am not a Christian*), B.C.Johnson (*The Atheist Debater's Handbook*), George H. Smith (*Atheism: The Case Against God*), and so many others have pointed out, their flaws have been, over the course of the last few centuries, revealed.

Consider the first cause argument: everything must be caused by something (nothing can come from nothing), therefore, God exists – God is the something that created everything, or at least that created everything that caused everything else. But who created God? No one: God is self-caused. Then why couldn't everything else, or even some of everything else, also be self-caused? You can't have your cake and eat it too: you can't say everything needs a cause in order to get to God and then suddenly change your mind (when you get to God) and say no, not everything needs a cause.

Consider the argument from design: when we observe the world, we see how everything fits together so nicely, it's obvious it was created, by design, by God. Well, one, you must be looking at different stuff: I observe that I don't have earlids. And two, even if I grant that everything does fit together very nicely, it's not obvious that it does so from design: it could be from adaptation (and what *didn't* fit together with everything else simply died).

There are many more, and equally poor, arguments for a God, but anyone who *really* wants to examine his/her belief can look them up. In short, there's no reason, no basis, for such belief.

But even if you *do* accept one of the arguments supporting belief in God, you still have to find a reason for believing in *your* god. Christians (the dominant group in Canada and the States) still have to find a reason for believing in the *Christian* God; Muslims still have to find a reason for believing in the Muslim God; etc.

The most common reason for believing in Jesus Christ *et al* is that 'It says so in *The Bible* and *The Bible* is the word of God.' This is circular; it's like saying you know that Santa Claus exists because he said he did in a letter he wrote to you – you believe he exists (you believe the letter was written by him) in order to prove that he exists.

Quite apart from the invalidity, let's consider consistency: it says a lot of other stuff in *The Bible* too. For example, if you do something wrong with your hand, you should cut it off (Matt 5:29-30); you shouldn't plan for the future (Matt 6:34); you shouldn't work to obtain food (John 6:27) – but my guess is you don't believe any of *that*. So if you're just going to pick and choose and believe only what you want to believe, why involve *The Bible* at all – why not just start from scratch?

Then there are those who believe in God because they had a vision, because God appeared to them. I can't deny personal experience. I can, however, point out that such a person's *interpretation* of their personal experience is unlikely and/or is inconsistent with a lot of other stuff (not the least of which is *other* people's personal experiences). And I can direct such people to a study of psychology and physiology, which would provide alternative explanations worth considering. (Ever wonder why such visions and conversions usually occur to people who already believe in God? And/or who are in a state of extreme stress or weakness?)

Let's face it: Christianity is a superstitious cult just like any other we so quickly condemn and then rush to save our children from. Unfortunately, because it's a cult that has brainwashed entire societies, from birth, it's safe from such criticism (and therefore more dangerous). Haven't you ever thought how coincidental it is that most people believe in the religion they were raised in? Doesn't that spell 'brainwash' to you? If people freely chose Christianity from among half a dozen others, at the age of maturity, with none having had a headstart, well, that would be different. And in that case, I doubt there would be so many Christians around.

And actually, I doubt that there are. So many Christians around. Except for fundamentalists, fanatics, and a few others who *do* choose in adulthood, who are 'born again', religion is less a belief than a habit. And habits are hard to break. Especially life-long habits that have become security blankets (if only because familiarity is comforting). Saying 'I believe in God' is such a life-long habit.

It's especially hard to break a habit if you think you need it. And most people mistakenly think religious belief is a prerequisite for morality. I think this explains the outrage at atheists: to say 'I don't believe in God' is thought to mean 'I'm immoral' or at least 'I'm amoral.' But let's be clear here. One, to be Christian entails a lot more than being good; and if Christians had the honesty to recognize that, frankly, they'd be acting differently – they would be cutting off their hands, or they'd be doing anything they want because all is forgiven, or they'd be in a deep depression because they did everything they wanted and are now damned to hell (did I mention that Christianity is full of contradictions?).

Two, being good does not require that you be Christian; it just requires that you have an ethical system. And there are several, in addition to Christian ethics, to choose from: values-based ethics, rights-based ethics, consequence-based ethics, etc. (And the key word there is *choose*.)

Next time you cross yourself or chant a prayer, consider the nature of superstition and habit.

---

1. "Whosoever shall not receive the kingdom of God as a little child shall in no wise enter therein" (Luke 18: 16-17) (Matthew says almost the exact same thing) (copycat).

Sex, like Religion / Religion, like Sex

What do Madonna, Prince, and Leonard Cohen [1] have in common – with evangelists, ministers, and priests? They all feed on the proximity of religion and sex.

But, but, you stutter, don't religions mostly prohibit sex, considering pretty much anything to do with the body to be distasteful or unclean or just plain immoral? Well, yes. Could be hypocrisy. Could be denial.

So what can religion and sex possibly have in common? Well, they both promise transcendence, ecstasy. (They both fail to deliver, but that's another point.)

What else? Religion is like infatuation (which is fuelled by sexual desire): both involve adoration, worship, of the object of one's desire. Add a little confusion and pretty soon one deifies the object of one's desire or desires the object of one's deification.

And both religion and sex involve salvation: one looks to God like one does to a lover, for salvation in the other's arms. (They both fail to – never mind.)

Furthermore, sex involves a release, a purging if you like – rather like fasting, or confessing and then doing penance. Again, one gets confused with the other, and pretty soon sex is thought to purify. I'm sure that's what all those priests thought when they had sex with those boys. Consider the sadomasochism and bondage and discipline. More than one saint has submitted to flagellation, by self or by others. Isn't every monk given a hairshirt and every nun her own little whip?

And on that note – it's no coincidence that 'rape' and 'rapture' come from the same root.

---
1. And no doubt so many other, more current, ones …

I Don't Have a Conscience

While I was very pleased, way back in 1997, to see the introduction of Bill C-272 regarding the use of taxes for military purposes, I was not at all pleased with its title: The Conscientious Objection Act. I object to paying for a lot of weaponry, but I don't have a conscience.

Phrases such as "Follow your conscience" and "Do what your conscience tells you" suggest that one's conscience is a fixed sort of thing, an unchanging absolute. Indeed, it often sounds like one's conscience is innate, something we're born with. And something quite separate from us, a sort of homunculus, or at least an 'inner voice' (the voice of God?). Chomsky may have proven that there are innate structures of language in the human brain, but to date, to my knowledge, no one has proven there are, in the human brain, innate moral principles. Nor, despite a dictionary definition of conscience as "the moral *sense* of right and wrong", has such a sixth (?) sense been established.

On the contrary, our 'conscience' is acquired: it is the collection of moral principles, or more accurately, since the acquisition occurs before we have the cognitive competence to handle *principles*, it is the collection of moral *habits*, that have been inculcated during childhood. So our conscience is dependent on our parents' moral principles, or, more likely, habits, and to some extent on the principles manifested by our community, our society. Our conscience amounts to nothing more than a moral reflex. We say "Examine your conscience", but we do not intend a critical examination; rather, we mean a simple examination of discovery. We never say "*Develop* your conscience"' or, God forbid, "*Reconsider* your conscience".

And yet surely that's what our attitude toward moral

principles should be: moral principles should not be inherited by indoctrination, but developed and maintained by careful, rational thought. I propose therefore that we replace the word 'conscience' with 'ethics'. 'Ethics' refers not to one's *sense* but to one's *system* (hopefully it's a system, a coherent collection) of moral principles. Bill C-272 should be called "The Ethical Objection Act" – for all of us who object, on *ethical* grounds, to the use of taxes for the military.

Now many people may be reluctant to replace 'conscience' with 'ethics' because, well, whose ethics? But that's exactly the question that must be asked. And it should be asked of conscience as well. I suspect there's a rather naive presumption of homogeneity with respect to conscience: when someone advises you to follow your conscience, my guess is that the person assumes you will choose to do the right thing, which is the same right thing he or she would do. But what if my conscience tells me to torture? What is the response to that – 'Your conscience must be wrong'? Until we ask *whose ethics*, we're avoiding the issue, skating on the thin ice of individual relativism, the very weakest of ethical systems: X is right because I think it's right (I followed my conscience). It's circular and most unhelpful: Why do you think it's right? How do you come to that thought? That is, *what makes you think it's right?* (Where did you get your conscience from?)

The fear, of course, is that the question has no answer, that we will set ourselves adrift on a sea of cultural relativism. Not true: we're capable of making anchors. We must confront the fact that we decide what's right and wrong, and surely deciding consciously is better than deciding unconsciously. Surely it is better to identify and compare, to critique, to evaluate, to choose our moral principles. And then to act, and lobby, according to those principles, instead of merely according to our 'conscience'.

Our Christian Language

I hadn't really thought about it until I saw 'his word' corrected to 'His Word' on a Writing Competency Test at a publicly-funded university.

I can accept a capital on 'God' because the word is being used as a name, and names are generally capitalized. (Though I do find it rather presumptuous to so appropriate a common noun. It's also a bit coercive: to use a common noun without an article is to imply there's only one – the claim 'Cat is happy' demands the question '*Which* cat?' *unless* you think there's only one; so when the rest of us want to refer to the Christian god, since we must say 'God' instead of using a real name like 'Zeus' or 'Hela', we are unwillingly implying the same belief.)

And I can accept capitals on '*The Bible*', as well as italics, because the words refer to the title of a book, and such words are generally capitalized, as well as italicized.

But what's the rationale for capitalizing 'His Word'? It was suggested to me, when I questioned the marking committee, that 'his word' was being used to refer to *The Bible* and so, as a title, should be capitalized. Well, one, then it should also be italicized, and, oddly, this wasn't mentioned. Two, we generally don't accept substitute titles for other books; for example, we would not accept *The Dictionary* for *The Concise Oxford Dictionary* – not at the university level.

I suspect the student meant 'his word' not as an equivalent to *The Bible*, but as an equivalent to 'his teaching'. So again, what's the rationale for capitals? With two exceptions, no other pronoun is ever capitalized.

The first exception is that pronouns are capitalized when they refer to royalty – 'His Majesty'. I suspect it's meant to show respect. Well I, for one, don't respect someone who's in a position of power and wealth merely by accident of birth. And for our language rules to impose such a display of respect is completely unjustified.

The second exception is 'I'. This one's unjustified on the grounds of inconsistency alone: no other subject pronoun is capitalized in the normal course of things. To make 'I' an exception is to be egocentric as well as inconsistent.

Since both exceptions are then, to my mind, unjustified, neither, to my mind, supports capitalizing in the instance under consideration. So much for 'his' in 'his word'.

As for 'word' (or 'teaching' or 'messages' or whatever), it doesn't belong to *any* class of nouns usually capitalized (names of people, countries, cities, months, etc.). Case closed.

So capitalizing 'His Word' seems to be an *exception* to the rules. And on what basis is this exception made? Well, it seems to me that capitalizing 'His Word' is meant to designate some special status, some special respect. And, as I suggested when I considered 'His Majesty', language has no business legislating opinions of value.

More specifically, religious values have no place in our grammatical rules. It especially has no place in the grammatical rules taught in public schools. Jewish schools can teach their kids to write 'G-d' and Christian schools can teach their kids to write 'His Word' – but neither should be stipulated as a common rule of grammar, and students in public schools should not be 'corrected' if they don't express these religious opinions through their spelling.

Nor should such rules be in any grammar book not identified as a Christian grammar book. Lamentably, five out of five grammar texts that I checked listed as a rule that names of deities and other religious names and terms be capitalized. However, in three at least, capitalizing the pronoun was presented as optional.

It's one thing to impose religious belief in public education

[1], which is not only contrary to the view that a just society is one which separates Church and State, but also contrary to the view that public education is committed to the pursuit of knowledge, not superstition.

It's another, and far more insidious, thing to entrench religious belief in our common language. We've exposed the sexism rooted in our language, and we have managed to begin to make changes. It's past time to do the same for the religionism rooted in our language. Just as B.C. (Before Christ) has given way to B.C.E. (Before the Common Era), let's make 'His Word' and the like equally anachronistic.

---

1. For example, through insisting that all students in public schools stand and recite the Lord's Prayer [sic] every morning.

Acts of God

Calling tornadoes, hurricanes, floods, and so forth 'acts of God' exempts insurance companies, and sometimes individuals, from responsibility.

Fair enough. Then let's sue the responsible party. Let's sue God.

If he doesn't show up, maybe people will start thinking he doesn't exist. Maybe they'll stop believing that he does.

And if he does show up, well, what's he going to say? That he didn't know about the tornado? There goes omniscience.

That he did know, but couldn't do anything about it? There goes omnipotence.

That he did know, and he could've done something, but – chose not to. There goes benevolence.

No doubt some believer in the courtroom will protest, 'God works in mysterious ways.' Try us.

Maybe God himself will protest, 'Who are you to presume to question me?' Um, we're your children. (No doubt someone will figure out that that makes him the son of god.)

It can't end well. God will be on the hook for compensation. It'll set a precedent. It might even require back-compensation. (What's the statute of limitations for acts of God?) Everyone who's ever suffered personal injury or property damage from a storm or lightning-triggered forest fire ... my God! He'd have to restore their belongings, their houses, their – lives.

Then *I'd* believe.

Appropriation or Imagination?

Two poems of mine have been published in a journal dedicated to "the Black experience". An audio piece of mine has been aired on First Nations radio programs. I am neither Black nor a member of any First Nation. Had this been known, I suspect some might have accused me of cultural appropriation.

It's an interesting idea, but as a reincarnation of the autobiographical school of writing – according to which one must have actually experienced what one is writing about – it is also a poor idea.

Taken to its logical extreme, any poem about a child must have been written by a child. Well no, one could say, you were *at one time* a child, so that's okay. Hm. So memory is okay but imagination is not? I suggest that often the one is as accurate as the other.

But perhaps accuracy is not the point. Perhaps it's a matter of "I can speak for myself, thank you" – a reaction against previous patronizing attitudes to the contrary. And if that's the case, if you *can* speak for yourself, then by all means do so. But that shouldn't stop me from *also* doing so if I want to. And if the editor or publisher selects only and always *my* speaking, then take that up with the editor or publisher, not the writer. Let's be inclusive rather than reactionarily exclusive.

Further, there is a difference between speaking *for* and speaking *about*. Speaking *for* does entail the suggestion of advocacy – patronizing if unrequested, and possibly unnecessary. Speaking *about* entails no such suggestion. And actually, there's a third option, the one that I thought I was doing – speaking *with*.

Think, for a moment, of all the literature that would not exist if writers had to limit themselves to what they have personally experienced. Entire genres would disappear: science fiction, speculative fiction, fantasy, historical fiction, probably most adventure and mystery too. Oh, and romance.

Also, to be consistent, this perspective should extend to non-fiction writing as well. So there goes most of the news – most stories are not first-hand accounts. But at least, you'll say, the third person accounts remain third person – there is no saying 'I' when you really mean 'he/she'. True. And this is one important difference between fiction and non-fiction – the leap of the imagination, the projection of oneself into the other.

But let's not pretend for even one second that news reports are bereft of this very same imagination. If they were, they'd have to be written in a purely phenomenological fashion, bereft of *all* ascriptions of emotion, for starters. To say 'the demonstrators were angry' instead of 'the demonstrators were shouting' is as much a leap of imagination – unless the reporter spoke to the demonstrators (all of them) and they said they were angry. (Even then, strict accuracy requires you to report 'they said they were angry' rather than 'they were angry'.) To merely assume anger on the basis of their behaviour is to project, to imagine, to fictionalize. Chances are, you're quite correct, they *were* angry. If you know about human behaviour and if you know about the context, you can probably come up with a very accurate story without actually experiencing it yourself. *The same goes for the fiction writer.* (But then again, I suspect accuracy is not the issue.)

Furthermore, the 'no appropriation' perspective doesn't seem to recognize that there are people whose awareness doesn't go very deep. They live in and for the moment, they are not reflective, they are not analytic. Or they may be all that but just not very articulate. And there are others whose research is thorough, whose imagination is rich, and who are articulate to boot. Which is why Brian Moore can write a better novel about a woman with PMS than a woman who has it but doesn't even know it. And which is why I can write a better poem about being Black or a First Nations person than some Blacks or First Nations people can. In short, one's imagination can exceed another's awareness.

But it's not really 'just' imagination, it's *informed* imagination – it's *empathy*. So not only does the 'no appropriation' perspective discourage imagination, it discourages empathy. But surely to limit ourselves to ourselves is sad. And dangerous.

Cultural Anarchy

Why is it that so many people claim, usually with considerable passion, "I'm an American!" or "I'm Canadian" or what have you?

To identify yourself by country is to accept the territorial divisions made by people with economic power eager to retain that power. So why the passion? Furthermore, why grant such importance to an accident of birth? You had nothing to do with where you were born.

To identify yourself by the country in which you happened to be born is bad enough, but to identify yourself by the country in which your parents or grandparents or greatgrandparents were born, as many do ("I'm African-American" and "I'm Japanese-American"), according to the birthplace of people you may not even have known, people who are long dead, is worse. Why is where your grandparents were born so much more important than what you think, what you value, and what you do? Why wouldn't you identify yourself *that* way? "I'm an atheist" or "I'm an environmentalist" or "I'm a painter." Identification by country of ancestral origin smacks of tribalism. [1]

For some people, such identity claims are a matter of culture, not country. But what *is* culture? What exactly *is* cultural identity? Race, religion, and nation are often used almost interchangeably to define culture: consider 'I'm Black', 'I'm Christian', and 'I'm Chinese-Canadian'; consider 'I'm Jewish' which is, apparently, a bit of all three.

First, insofar as cultural identity is *racial* identity, it must, again, depend on an accident of birth, on chance, on something you did not consent to: we do not choose our race – we do not choose the colour of our skin, the shape of our eyes, the bridge of our nose, the fullness of our lips, etc.

Second, insofar as cultural identity is *religious* identity, and insofar as religion is a system of beliefs, it is, at least, *not* an accident of birth: one cannot be *born* a Catholic, for example, because one cannot be born believing anything, one simply doesn't have the cognitive capacity at birth to form beliefs. But that kind of cultural identity is, then, something you can have only as an adult, when you have developed the intellectual faculty capable of understanding, assessing, and choosing beliefs.

Third, insofar as cultural identity is *national* identity, we are, barring emigration, back to an accident of birth and an endorsement of political 'agreements'.

Perhaps, rather than defining culture as a matter of race, religion, or nationality, it is better defined as a collection of costumes and customs, mere habits, practices, a way of living. But it seems strange to elevate your habits to the status of an identity, and then, perhaps, to demand certain rights on the basis of those habits.

What about defining culture as a set of values? This would certainly make race and nation irrelevant: values are seldom clearly correlated with racial or national boundaries – to say 'I'm Black' or 'I'm Serbian' doesn't necessarily say anything about your values, let alone anything exclusive or exhaustive. While your religious identity more probably does say something about your values, it would also be irrelevant because, again, it says nothing exclusive or exhaustive – a Muslim and a non-Muslim may both value X, and a Muslim may have values additional to those of the Islamic religion. And in any case, I question the individual who accepts so totally the set of values held by, presumably, a race, nation, or religion. Culture is not indelibly imprinted. To be a feminist is proof of that.

Another interpretation of culture refers to group history, the group involved being a group in which membership depends on some kind of heritage. But why should history, heritage, constitute identity? Why should our past define your present? More important, why should *someone else's* past define your present? Why should a *group's* past define an *individual's* present? One possible reason might be in order to avenge and/or to ensure compensation. But to make someone pay for the 'sins' of his or her ancestors is ridiculous. What my greatgrandfather did or didn't do has nothing to do with me; I didn't even know the man. [2]

A second reason for making group history the basis of one's cultural identity might be in order to preserve what's of value. Surely this is important, but why limit yourself to the lessons of your own group? And while there may be value in being custodians of the past, why should the job be open only to those with a direct genetic line of descent? Why can't I carry the torch for a tradition I value *whether or not* anyone in my bloodline also carried it? [3]

Country of birth, race, ancestral religion, group history – I find it difficult to understand why people choose to identify themselves by such accidents of birth. That I am 5'4" is accidental – I had no choice in the matter and I have no control over it. So why would I choose to trumpet my height as my identity? It seems to me that there is something fundamentally irrational about claiming as your identity aspects of your self that are mere accidents of birth: if you don't choose X, if you have no control over X, then surely you can't justifiably take any credit or blame for X – nor, then, can you take any of the attendant benefits and burdens. It's also a very passive thing, basing your identity on what chance has done to you rather than on what you've done yourself. Perhaps most importantly, it's also unfair, if rights and responsibilities are assigned on such an identity.

Whether we admit it or not, we do choose our practices, our beliefs, and our values. And to identify ourselves according to such rational bases is to be responsible for ourselves. And cultural anarchy, assimilation and appropriation at will, enables, indeed reflects, this choice.

    1. I can see that identity claims according to ancestral lineage ("I'm First Nations because my greatgrandfather was First Nations") are important in many territorial conflicts, but they're typically based on arguments of primacy – which are flawed on at least three counts. One, what does it matter who was here first? Does mere presence entitle one to ownership? Doesn't the quality of one's presence matter at all?

    Two, what time shall we establish as the starting point, and on what basis shall we establish it as the starting point? For example, certainly the various indigenous tribes were here before the Europeans (and so "I have a right to X, a greater right to X than you, that is, because my ancestors were here before your ancestors"), but the various indigenous tribes also came from somewhere else 10-50,000 years ago – so they're not really indigenous. They're not *native*, they're just *prior*. To be fair, we'd have to determine the time and location of each evolution into homo sapiens (should this be a measurable moment) and then establish complete lineages, in order to determine whose ancestors were where first. (Unless, of course, we just accept the Judeao-Christian view – in which case everyone not currently living in whatever country the Garden of Eden was in is an immigrant, not indigenous, a non-native.)

    Three, even if we accept a right of primacy, on what grounds do we include that right in one's genetic heritage? What my greatgrandfather did or didn't do has nothing to do with me – I should not pay for his errors, nor should I have the right to go back to his childhood home (should I be able to determine where it is) and demand to be paid for what was stolen from him. It was stolen from *him*, not from *me*. What is his is his, not mine. Unless, I suppose, he left a will stating that whatever it was that was stolen was to have been given to me. But even then, one could reasonably argue that what is merely *potentially* yours isn't yours enough to warrant a charge of theft should such theft cause that potential not to be actualized. And he could have as easily willed that it be given to the greatgrandson of a friend. (Perhaps likely, given the sexism of many inheritance traditions.) Why are genetics so very important? What if, after all, I'm adopted? (And therefore don't even have the same skin colour as my greatgrandfather?)

2. An exception would be if descendents suffer the consequences of the wrongs done to, or the privileges awarded to, their ancestors. But not only does this assume an inheritance that may or may not have occurred (see note 1), it is incredibly complex and ultimately uncertain: how can we really know for sure which aspects of one's present are due to which aspects of another's past?

3. This raises the issue of assimilation and appropriation: why do they have such bad reps? After all, isn't conditioning, isn't education, merely assimilation? Weren't we assimilated (i.e., encouraged to conform to the customs and values) into our first cultural group, the one we belong to by birth? Why the foofarah when we are re-assimilated, into a second cultural group, the one we *choose*? And isn't appropriation merely adopting – the customs, practices, beliefs, values, and so on of some group? And what's wrong with that? (Frankly, it's unlikely one would adopt the whole set, since it's likely to be internally inconsistent, but that's another point ...)

Government Grants for Grad School to First Nations People

So a colleague at work, another part-timer, who's also going to grad school this September, got a government grant. She'll be getting $675/month to cover her living expenses. I've spent five years saving $10,000 to cover my living expenses (hopefully it won't take more than ten months to get my degree).

She's 'native'. Well, she was born in Canada same as me, actually in the same year even, but her parents' parents' parents' parents' parents' parents were living here before the Europeans moved in.

So, the argument goes, the money is compensation for past prejudice. Okay, then let's *establish* past prejudice. I mean, how exactly were her parents and grandparents denied opportunities – that, presumably, my parents and grandparents were not?

She tells me that in high school, she got 50s and 60s. So? She also tells me that she was delinquent. Excuse me, but that's her fault. How can it be her parents' parents' parents' fault? Did what the Europeans do (deny them jobs?) somehow create a culture of laziness among the people who were here first? And they were powerless to resist that? I attended school every fucking day, did all my homework, and then some, and got 80s and 90s. I guess because I'm white. And lower middle-class. Bullshit!! There were plenty others like me who skipped. And got 50s and 60s. My brother, for one.

But I was encouraged, she explains. She wasn't, because school isn't important in the native culture. Yes, I was expected to go to school every day. And my parents were happy, though not particularly enthusiastic about, my grades, but that's about it. I wouldn't say I was encouraged. In fact, I was *dis*couraged from pursuing a graduate degree in Philosophy.

If she attended every class, and did all her homework, and then some, and scored well on a culture bias-free IQ test, and *still* got 50s and 60s, then I'd say, yeah, okay, she's a victim of prejudice.

But even if that were the case, how does $675/month compensate for the prejudice? How does it equal my privilege? I got As, but that didn't lead to $675/month. I ended up with the same part-time job she did (she's a colleague, remember?). The same number of shifts, at the same rate of pay. If she had applied for the same jobs as me and *not* gotten them in spite of similar qualifications and experience (and opportunity to get said qualifications and experience), then I'd say, yeah, okay, unfair discrimination.

But still, why just give her $675/month? Wouldn't it make more sense to give her a job that pays $675/month? Doesn't the hand-out just repeat the past, which presumably is at fault, for putting her in this awful present of hers?

Taxing the Rich

Of course the rich people should have to pay higher taxes. Not because of some 'trickle down' principle or some 'sacrifice for the common good' principle or some 'from each according to their ability' principle, but because they don't deserve their money. There, I said it. They don't deserve their millions.

Even if I worked twenty hours a day, 365 days of the year, I wouldn't make anywhere near just one million.

So they must be making ten, twenty, a hundred times per hour what I'm making.

Is what they're doing a hundred times more important than what I'm doing. It's not even ten times more important. (Let's say I'm a garbage collector.)

Is it a hundred or ten times more difficult? No. (Let's say I'm a nurse in the paraplegic ward.)

Does it take a hundred or ten times as much skill or training? No. (Let's say I'm an astrophysicist.)

Rich people have their millions because they've been paid, by others or by themselves, an unfair amount for their work. Or because they know how to work an unfair economic system that, for starters, rewards risk: the stock market.

But why do we reward risk? Because it's a male thing. And males reward themselves for male values.

Actually, though, often it's not a risk. If the company they started, the company they invested in, lost millions, they could declare bankruptcy. And *other* people would pay the price. Not them. Or if they're really big, if they lost really big, the government might bail them out. That is, us.

Furthermore, they're not even risking *their own* money. They probably borrowed the start-up money from the bank. So it's our money. Or the bank's money (which is just money *they* made by investing *our* money).

Or if it *was* their own money, well it still wasn't. It was inherited from their parents. (Who probably inherited it from *their* parents). Because you can't *have* that much money to invest by working and saving. Even if you work twenty hours a day, 365 days a year …

Private Property and Visual Intrusion

There should be regulations about what people can put on their private property that will be in view of their neighbours. Even more than in public spaces, visual material on private property is not easily avoided. If you put a swastika or a pornographic image on your garage door, and that door is right across from your neighbours' living room window, they will have to see it every time they look out their window. Asking them not to look out their window is unreasonable. If you were there first and had the image on your garage door when they were looking for a place, they could have chosen to not move in (and so don't have the right to ask you to remove it) (maybe). But if they were there first, they have a right to ask you not to put the image on your garage door.

But it's not even, or not only, so-called 'offensive' images that I'd prohibit. It's *anything* the neighbour doesn't want to see every day, anything that's *an unwanted intrusion on their consciousness*. It could be a 'Jesus Loves You' sign (unwanted by the atheist), the Canadian flag (upsetting to someone who is well aware of Canada's environmental record), or even an inoffensive and non-upsetting image of an infant playing with building blocks. Who knows? It doesn't matter. The people who are forced to see your house every day are the ones who get a say in how it looks. From the outside. To them. What you put in your back yard doesn't affect them, so they don't have a say. What you put inside your garage, or inside your house, doesn't affect them, so they don't have a say. But what you put in plain view? They should have a say. A reasonable say.

Obviously the effects of such a prohibition increase the more visible you are. If you own a penthouse apartment that can be seen by thousands, guess what. If you own a house on a lake that can be seen by everyone on the lake, guess what.

To provide just one example, I live in a cabin on a lake in a forest and several people consider it appropriate to 'decorate' their property, lakeside, with solar lights that can never be turned off. Some are arranged in a runway fashion to mark a path from their house to their lake; some are arranged in a row along their frontage. Needless to say, the lights really ruin the beauty of the lovely moonlight glimmering on the water, the otherwise dark forest … I claim that such lights shouldn't be allowed.

First, my right to revel in the natural beauty every night trumps their right to 'decoration' *that isn't even being appreciated* (if they're weekenders, they're back in the city during the week and so don't see their lights; if they live there, they're typically asleep in bed after midnight and so don't see their lights). Second, my right to revel in the natural beauty trumps the marginal utility of the lights even when they *are* there or awake *because there are alternatives* (one can use a flashlight or install motion sensor lights that go on only when one needs to see the way). People with lakeside solar lights are imposing their conception of decoration and utility on everyone else, and they are preventing others from appreciating their own conception of beauty (the dark night, the moonlight glimmering on the water). If your property is in the middle of natural beauty, you have an obligation not to ruin it. And if you don't see that, you shouldn't live there. Similarly, people who don't appreciate Beethoven shouldn't go to concerts and talk all the way through.

And if those lights are blinking, it's even worse: given the way our brains are wired, *our attention is coerced*. No one has a right to force me to pay attention to something I don't want to attend to, and blinking lights do just that.

One may counter by claiming that surely one is allowed to do what one wants on and with one's own property. Well, no. For example, you shouldn't be allowed to dump oil on your property – because it will seep through the soil into other people's property and into the lake. *When your actions affect others, there are limits to what you can do.*

In short, even though your property is 'private', what you put on it is not: as long as it can be seen by others, it's public. And it should therefore be subject to restrictions: you don't have a right to coerce other people's attention, especially if what you're forcing them to pay attention to is something they don't want to pay attention to.

Noise Trespass

We need a noise trespass law. At the very least, the concept of noise trespass should be as familiar among the general population as physical trespass.

Why is going onto someone's private property without permission (physical trespass) considered a wrong? Because doing so is intrusive (presuming a right to privacy) and potentially damaging. The same goes for sending noise onto someone's private property.

Noise is intrusive because it – the sound of machinery, loud music, screaming kids, even conversations (having to listen to someone have an extended cellphone conversation, for example) – detracts and distracts from whatever one is trying to do, whether that's watching TV, listening to (one's own preferred) music, writing an essay, filling out income tax returns, sleeping … it doesn't really matter. Surely we have a right to privacy concerning our attention; noise hijacks our attention – it coerces us to pay attention to something we don't want to pay attention to.

Noise is potentially damaging in a number of ways. Depending on a number of factors (of which dB is only one), noise "damages hearing [at least 20% of teenagers now suffer from slight hearing loss], disturbs communication, disrupts sleep, affects heart function, intrudes on cognition … , reduces productivity, provokes unwanted behaviors, and increases accidents" (Mitra). It can also cause or contribute to "anxiety, stress, nervousness, nausea, headache, emotional instability, argumentativeness, sexual impotence, change in mood, increase in social conflicts, neurosis, hysteria, and psychosis" (Noise Free America).

Noise produced by industry, airports, and so on is already

being monitored and regulated. I'm talking here about the noise caused by individuals in residential neighborhoods. Various sound charts put city traffic at around 80dB, the subway at 88dB, a garbage truck at 100dB; lawnmowers and leafblowers can be just as high, at 100dB (and last for half an hour, not just a few minutes), and chainsaws, dirt bikes, ATVs, boat motors, and PWCs are louder still, at around 110dB.

But, one might object, although we own our own property, and so have a right to object when someone trespasses on it, we don't own the air over our property, and sound travels through the air. There are several replies to this: we shouldn't own the land either (and yet physical trespass might still be wrong, merely because of occupancy); we should also own the air over our land (in which case, noise trespass is as wrong as physical trespass); we collectively own the air (and that's sufficient to consider noise a trespass); ownership is irrelevant altogether (occupancy is sufficient). People get upset when a neighbour's dandelion seeds travel through air and land on their property; is there not similar justification for getting upset when a neighbour's sound waves travel through air and 'land' – ah, but they don't land on one's property. No, but they 'land' on one's eardrums: sound is not perceived until the sound waves 'hit' one's eardrums. Surely that's even *more* intrusive: the sound waves actually touch our *body*, not just our property.

In any case, smoke from burning tires travels through air, and if it travels from your neighbour's property *through the air* onto your property, or, more accurately, into the air *over* your property, perhaps even through your open windows into your house, you would, I think, cry foul.

In addition to the intrusion and the damage, most of the annoying noise caused by individuals is avoidable. Manual lawnmowers, rakes, and clippers have enabled people to take care of their lawns for almost a century. I suspect that dirt bikes,

ATVs, and PWCs can be redesigned to be quiet; for starters, could they not use electric motors rather than two-stroke gas-powered motors? They certainly don't have to be modified to *increase* their noise (as they often are), and they can be driven in a fashion that minimizes their noise (as they often are not). And, of course, people could use, *instead,* bicycles, kayaks, canoes, and so on. And landline phones could be used (*inside*).

All of which begs the question: why *don't* we consider noise trespass to be trespass? Are we so unable to consider the invisible and the intangible? It we can't see it or touch it, it doesn't exist? Despite its obvious effects?

Or is it that men *like* noise? (After all, for the most part, they're the ones making it.) And it is the male view, male interests, male values that dictate law and custom, make no mistake about that. This is the view presented at Manly Power Tools. It's also the view endorsed by a certain electronic composer who, when asked why he writes such loud, dense music, replied "Besides the obvious? The desire to fill all this space with sound?" Perhaps men are still being led around by their primitive brain, and all their noise is just a sublimated roar, mistakenly believed to be necessary for survival. (Which begs the question: when will they evolve into *homo sapiens*?)

On Power Outages

I live in a cabin on a lake in the forest (which you'll know, if you're reading these pieces in order). You'd think that whenever the power goes out, there would be silence. Lovely silence. (And lovely dark.) And there is. For all of thirty seconds. Then everyone's backup generator goes on. And for the next five, ten, twenty, or forty-eight hours, I hear engine noise. Constant engine noise. Like a tractor trailer is parked in my driveway. Idling. Loudly.

Because my god but the world would end if people had to go without TV for five hours! Or without whatever the hell it is they need their generators for.

Two hours in, and they're driving into town. Because 'What about supper?' What? Food is that foremost on your mind? You're not in Ethiopia. You just ate a couple hours ago. And if you're really that hungry, don't you have *anything* in the house that can be eaten raw, out of the box, or out of the can?

Perhaps they can't stand the silence. No, that can't be right, because everyone's generators are on.

Is it that they can't stand the severance from – what, exactly? Civilization? Please. Most people here couldn't care less about their neighbours. When I asked one to join a sort of neighbourhood watch so we could call the fire department whenever, during a total fire ban, some asshole one had a huge, blazing campfire, as was his habit, she refused. Didn't want to stick her neck out.

Quite apart from the fact that a power outage doesn't sever you from civilization. Can't you hear everyone's generators? Everyone's still here.

Is it that people are so fearful they need the illusion of safety that noise and light provide? Hm. Now I understand why people have their TV on all day even though they aren't watching it. And it suddenly occurs to me that most of the people who live here never leave their houses, except to get into their car and go somewhere. I never see them out for a walk, on the road, or in the forest. I never see them down at the water, let alone out on the lake. (Why do they live here?)

Or perhaps it's just that there's nothing going on inside their little heads, so they need the external stimulation to keep them from utter boredom.

Far more than pathetic, it's scary. That people are so dependent on that kind of (external) energy.

An Open Letter to Weekenders Everywhere

This is not "a recreational paradise" or "a summer playground". This is our neighbourhood. Those labels are marketing ploys used by real estate agents and business owners eager to make money on sales. They do not speak for us. We live here; they do not.

Many of us have lived here for five, ten, twenty years. Half of us are retired; half of us still work. We live here because we want to live on a lake in a forest. We love to look out at the water and see the sun sparkle, the moonlight shimmer. We love to hear the birds and see the squirrels at our feeders; we stand in awe when we see the occasional moose or bobcat. We sit out in the evening and look up at the starry sky. We open our windows at night to hear the loons as we fall asleep. We love the peace and quiet; we bask in the solitude.

When you weekenders come here, you're not leaving the city and driving to a place where you can 'let loose' – you're simply leaving your own neighbourhood and entering ours. So when you do whatever the hell you want when you're here, of course we consider it an invasion. And of course we want our neighbourhood back.

When we have asked, politely, that you not drive so fast in your pick-ups, we were told we don't own the road. (And to prove it, you sped up as you passed us, spraying gravel in our faces.) When we have asked, politely, that you not come so close to us, paddling or swimming, on your jetskis, you have screamed at us "You don't own the fucking lake!" True enough. But this is not a public campground: it was not empty before you arrive, it does not exist solely for your pleasure. Did you really think no one lives here?

Right. Okay.

Churn up the roads with your ATVs; no one will have to deal with the grooves and gullies until the grader next comes by because no one lives here.

Drive around wherever you want, on the roads, on the trails. (Make new trails if you feel like it.) Do this all day. Because there isn't anyone within ten miles to hear you.

Don't worry about people having to walk through the fume trails you leave because no one but you ever wants to use the trails.

Leave your empty beer cans and coffee cups and cigarette butts and fast food cartons along the roads and trails. No one will see any of it because no one lives here.

Don't bother taking your household garbage to the dump; just toss it. Sure, it'll attract the bears, but you won't be putting anyone at risk because no one lives here.

(And when all of it's gone by the next time you're up, that's because a bunch of little elves came in the middle of the night and cleaned up after you.)

Use those environmentally-friendly solar lights that don't have an on-off switch. Put dozens all over your property; they'll stay on even when you're not here. But they won't spoil the dark and beautiful night, all night, every night, because no one lives here.

Have a campfire even when there's a fire ban. If the fire spreads, that's fine, no one's home will burn down, because no one lives here.

When you turn on the radio, turn it up loud. Open your windows. Better yet, put the radio outside. You won't be forcing anyone else to listen to it because no one lives here. (And if they did, rest assured they like exactly the same music you do and want to listen to it when and for as long as you do.)

Park your party barge in front of someone's house – oops, that's not someone's house. No one lives there. They won't hear your kids' shrieks or your loud conversations. (And if they do, they will care deeply about whether you remembered to buy marshmallows, where you left your hat, how to do a proper dive, whether the water's too cold, and what to say to Mark when you get back.)

You can also park your fishing boat in front of someone's house – oops. No one will smell your cigarette smoke or your motor fumes. They won't hear your conversations either. (And if they do, they will surely want to know that John's a fuckin' asshole and that you couldn't care less what that bitch does.)

Zoom around on your jetskis, and your large-motored boats, consider the lake an abandoned gravel pit, pretend you're doing the Indy 500. No one will have to go inside and shut their windows, because no one lives here.

Believe Home Depot and Canadian Tire when they tell you that being at the lake on the weekend is all about being a he-man: use all the power tools you want – nail guns, two-speed drills, circular saws, lawn mowers, weed trimmers, leaf blowers, and chain saws. Use them all outside. Use them on the lake side. Use them in the morning, in the afternoon, in the evening. No one will hear any of it because no one lives here. (And if they do, they don't want to sit outside anyway. It's not like they've been waiting through six months of winter and another month of bugs to finally be able to do so.)

Don't spend the money to hook up to hydro; use a generator instead. No one will have to hear the motor echo across the lake all day, and all evening, and into the night if you go into town and don't come back until two or three in the morning, because no one lives here.

Making Certain Words Illegal

Hate speech. Libel. Slander. Threat. Intimidation. Blasphemy.

'Making words illegal violates our freedom of speech!' Of course it does. But that freedom, like many others, isn't absolute. Our freedoms are *limited* freedoms. They are limited by several things (philosopher Joel Feinberg identifies six liberty-limiting principles), one of which is the harm principle. That is, when our action harms another person or society in general, it is limited. It (perhaps) should be illegal.

'But speech isn't an action. I didn't *do* anything. I just said –' Saying is doing. Words are speech acts. They are *acts* of speech. And anyway, if the result is the same, does the method really matter?

'Yeah but the result *isn't* the same. Words can't hurt you.' Well, not physically, no. But they can cause psychological injury. [1] And there's the heart of the matter: should we make causing psychological injury illegal?

Actually, that's *not* the heart of the matter. Yes, we should, and we do. The crime of torture includes acts which inflict severe mental pain or suffering (*CCC* 269.1[1]) – but such acts must be committed *in order to obtain information*.

The heart of the matter is *when* should we make psychological injury illegal? In order to answer that question, we need to figure out what exactly is injurious about psychological injury. I can identify two kinds of injury that can result from speech acts.

First, they can cause pain; it hurts to be called whatever or told whatever.

Second, they can cause a loss. Consider insult. At the minimum, it's annoying, it's irritating, it pisses us off. That's life. But consider *ongoing* insult. That makes life harder; it's exhausting to deal with it, whether you confront it or ignore it, and so you have less energy to deal with other stuff. Such as the pursuit of your interests.

Not only is there a loss of energy, there can be a real loss of opportunity and freedom. [2] When blows to your self-esteem and confidence are ongoing, it's hard not to start believing the insults, and so you start to doubt your worth, your potential, you censor yourself, you limit your options. And of course this could, often does, have economic consequences. You may not pursue a high income career (by not taking any one of the many steps required). [3] Even if you don't believe the insults, you might censor yourself for fear of provocation and violence, and if that happens in the classroom or the workplace, it can affect your grades and your evaluations, which can lead, again, to limited opportunities. Threats, also 'just' words, are even more restricting: if someone has threatened to kill me, I'm less apt to go where, when, and how I usually go.

Both of these, pain and loss, lead us to the next issue: how severe does the injury have to be? For example, do insults cause pain or just discomfort? Are we talking about a little embarrassment or debilitating humiliation? As for the loss, do the insults distract us from our task of the moment or cripple us for life?

It's complicated. Physical blows tend to injure no matter how strong you are or how fit you are. But psychological blows, well, to some extent it depends on your emotional health (on how mature you are, how secure your ego is) and your cognitive health (how intelligent you are, how able you are to evaluate the truth of the words). The more fragile you are, the more devastated you will be when you're called an idiot.

In addition to the argument of psychological maturity, the argument of freedom of speech also provides support for legalizing insult. One might argue that the harm done by restricting freedom of speech is far greater than the good done by eliminating insult. Do we want a society full of people who cannot withstand any offense? Some women may still be socialized to accept the power and authority of men (all men, any man), but if such a woman does not outgrow that and become an independent mature adult, then *she* should pay the price of her immaturity, not the rest of us. The law should not protect her immaturity at our expense, at the expense of our freedom. I value my freedom of speech and accept the risk – in fact, request the right – to be offended. Offense, while it can damage, can also stimulate, challenge, and lead to growth. That said, the pervasiveness of the insult needs to be considered; *ongoing, relentless* insult (which women tend to get in our society) is beyond the offense I'm talking about here.

Furthermore, it is our thoughts, opinions, beliefs, values, and attitudes that determine whether certain words injure us, and we are responsible for our thoughts, opinions, beliefs, values, and attitudes. If your belief in some fairy tale god is such that your blood pressure hits the roof when I say "God doesn't exist" – really, am *I* to blame? So, to some extent, if we *are* injured by certain words, it's our own fault. The same applies to threats: for example, a threat uttered by someone who's holding a gun and has used it in the past is more likely to be believed and therefore more injurious than a threat uttered by someone who is stoned, giggling and gunless.

Of course it all comes down to the standard of reasonableness. It's reasonable to expect that the other person is not so frail that a gentle shove fractures the spine. Likewise, surely it's reasonable to expect that an insult or blasphemy doesn't send someone into emotional shock. Do we really need to *require, legally*, a minimum standard of physical and psychological health, on the one hand, and a minimum standard of care, on the other? Perhaps. In which case, a combination of intent ('I only meant to scare him, I didn't know he was phobic';

'I only meant to shove him, I didn't know he had a bone condition') and consequence (he needed to be sedated; he has a broken back) might determine whether certain words should be illegal. [4]

For this reason, I would exclude from the realm of the illegal words that provoke violence. Let the violence be illegal, yes, but the provocation for the violence? Please. If we expect people to steel themselves against psychological injury from words, surely we should also expect them to steel themselves against making a physically violent response to words. After all, the latter is surely more within our control than the former. [5]

Onto the next issue: does it matter whether the injury is done in private or public? Typically words in the public arena are considered more problematic because you can't avoid the public arena. You can't avoid the subway walls, for example, the same way you can avoid listening to a certain radio station or reading a certain magazine. However, spousal physical abuse, even though conducted in the private arena, is now considered illegal. Does this suggest that words spoken in the privacy of our homes should be as illegal as those written on the subway walls? Perhaps – if they are as severe as the physical abuse and if the person can't avoid them (that is, if they have nowhere else to go – which may well be the case if they have children or are children).

Does it matter whether the words are written or spoken? On the one hand, an insult in writing is easier to avoid (just don't read it), unless, of course, it's written in public. But on the other hand, often, especially if digitally written, it has a longer life.

Does it matter whether the words are specific or general? Consider 'You're a loser!' vs. 'Canadians are losers!' My guess is that the specific insult is more personally damaging. But maybe not. The general insults of slavery and porn have been quite injurious.

Does it matter whether the words in question are true? I'd argue that whether it turns out to be true or not, if there's good reason to believe a threat, and the threat is serious enough to cause serious emotional injury – a constant state of fear, for example – it should be illegal. As for insults, it seems to me that if it is true, it shouldn't be illegal to say it. And yet there seems to be something more wrong with a billboard that says "Jane Smith smells" than with one that says "John Smith rapes" – both are an invasion of privacy, but the latter is in the public interest: it's purpose is to prevent harm to others, so that trumps privacy.

Notwithstanding all of this, a major complication of criminalizing psychological injury from speech acts is establishing cause and effect. It's easier with physical injury and physical acts. Not only is establishing cause and effect easier, establishing severity is also easier. I'm tempted to suggest that that's because the physical is less complex than the psychological, but I suspect it's because we understand the physical more than we understand the psychological: we know all about the heart, the lungs, the nervous system, the sensory systems, the 206 bones in the body, but we have yet to catalogue every sneer, every smirk, the hundred ways of making eye contact …

Another possible explanation for the current discrepancy [6], between illegalizing psychological injury and physical injury, between illegalizing words and actions, is that in our society, the male mode (still) (sigh) rules. Certainly the lawmakers have traditionally been men. And men have, traditionally, spent more time in the physical arena than in the emotional arena. [7] So perhaps it is not surprising that physical hurts have received more attention than emotional hurts. [8]

Furthermore, men (more than women) engage in business, income-generating activities – making money is traditionally their role, their legitimator. So injuries to their income-generating activities is important; hence, the laws against libel and slander, words that damage their income-generating reputation. [9]

Further still, loss of income is more measurable than loss of self-esteem; as mentioned, physical injury is more measureable than psychological injury. And men are more engaged in, more comfortable with, quantitative activities than qualitative activities. They like measurement.

A final note, however, notwithstanding the previous discussion, is that physical aggression is considered illegal even when it doesn't injure. It's the action, not the consequence, that determines its illegality. If you punch me, whether I bruise, or break, or neither, I can still charge you with assault. Why doesn't insult have the same legal weight? Because unless there's money or a fight involved, men aren't into words?

---

1. Assuming, of course, a distinct separation between the physical and the psychological. And most current research indicates no such separation. Even without such research, we know that psychological states can affect our physical states (sorrow and stress make us tired) and physical states can affect our psychological states (running can make us happy.)
2. Certainly threat and intimidation will have this consequence.
3. Of course it's this kind of loss that makes libel and slander illegal. Both refer to false statements (libel, written; slander, oral) that injure a person's reputation, and you can bet that the reputation being talked about is that which enables the person to make money. Ditto fraud, misrepresentation and false advertising: money is at stake.
4. That said, the standard of reasonableness is fraught with difficulty, not the least of which is that what's a reasonable response for a woman, in our society, differs from that of a man. For example, women *reasonably* fear sexual violence in certain places at certain times; men do not. Another, more subtle, example, is that women, in our society, more reasonably believe what(ever) men say than vice versa.* These examples also expose the problem with using 'community standards' – which, whose, community? There are subcultures within cultures, each with their own framework of concepts and values …

That said, we enter a minefield when we *without question* consider group membership: being a woman or a man is more than a matter of anatomy – it's a matter of social construction; and socialization influences people to varying degrees – which woman, and which man, are involved? Further, society is fluid – it isn't either patriarchal or not patriarchal; sexism may be stronger or weaker at any given time and place, in any situation.

Also, we need to be careful not to assume that all women are unable to withstand all insult; that would more than infantalise them.

* Power, according to Hannah Arendt (*On Violence*), belongs to a group and is the instrument of rule. Strength belongs to the individual. Force, she defines, as "the energy released by physical or social movements" (p. 45). Lastly authority, vested in individuals or offices, is indicated by the "unquestioning recognition of those who are asked to obey; neither coercion nor persuasion is needed" (p. 45); "to remain in authority requires respect" (p. 45). Is it then that insults and threats have power and authority only (or moreso) when they are spoken by a man to a woman? They have power because the individual man is an automatic member of the ruling class in our society, and they have authority because women are 'asked to obey'; and they have strength as well because as an individual, he is a man. So the same insult, the same threat, from one man to another, or from one woman to another, is not (as) injurious, is not (as) violent?

5. I've always been suspicious of 'crimes of passion' and 'fighting words' – maybe it's just me, maybe it's just me being female, but I simply can't imagine what someone might say that would make me take a swing at them. Tell them to go to hell, yes, but hit them?

6. Which is changing: while the *Canadian Criminal Code* defines harassment such that fear for one's (physical) safety is required, the *Ontario Human Rights Code* defines it such that merely humiliation is required: "a course of comment or conduct consisting of words or actions that disparage or humiliate a person in relation to one of the prohibited grounds" (race, ancestry, place of origin, colour, ethnic origin, citizenship, creed, sex, sexual orientation, age, record of offense, marital status, family status, receipt of public assistance, and handicap); in fact, compensation may be awarded for the 'mental anguish' caused (rather than for any physical anguish).

7. Sports – physical contests – are typically dominant in their lives

8. After all, 'real' men don't even *have* emotions!

9. Consider that, especially compared to men, women don't have income-generating reputations. They *do* have sexual reputations. And yet, at the moment, I don't believe they can sue if some guy writes her name on the locker room wall …

"I killed you. Killed you too. Got you."
In the Library.

So I was working in my local public library the other day – well, *trying* to work. I was distracted by the kid on the computer next to me who was playing a computer game. My first point. Is it appropriate for kids to be allowed to play computer games on the computers in public libraries? I suggest that libraries are repositories of knowledge that people peruse to borrow or access on-site. Given that, playing computer games should not occur in a public library. Libraries aren't entertainment centers. [1] Yes, perusing and accessing knowledge can be fun. But that doesn't mean that that which is fun is necessarily perusing or accessing knowledge.

Furthermore, the kid was continuously commenting, not in a particularly loud voice, but certainly loud enough for me, sitting next to him, to hear. My second point. Goes along with the intense irritation I experienced while in the university library a few weeks ago, unable to search the stacks for what I was seeking (books containing arguments) because someone in one of the nearby carrels was talking on her cellphone. Not an emergency conversation, mind you, but a mundane hi-yeah-so-like-whatever one. Given that libraries are repositories of knowledge that one either peruses to borrow or accesses on site – both of which often require mental effort, requiring concentration, which is inhibited by the distraction of talking aloud – both the kid's running commentary and the cellphone conversation should not have occurred.

Further still, the kid's comments were "I killed you. Killed you too. Got you. Killed you." and so on. Not only distracting, but disturbing. My third point? Given that the library is indeed a *public* library, and not withstanding what I've said elsewhere, I think there may be grounds for censorship – could that be considered "hate speech" or "disturbing the peace"? It's bad enough that the kids' parents are irresponsibly unaware of the damage being done to their kids, not to mention to the rest of us, by allowing such activity (it desensitizes the kid to death, and it forms an association between killing and fun/entertainment), but there is no excuse for public librarians to be so unaware. And, given the public status (and funding) of the library, they have grounds for acting on their awareness.

---

1. But what about all that fiction? Okay, but isn't it generally 'serious literature' – fiction that has, presumably, insight – knowledge – about the human condition? Actually, no. Don't a lot of libraries have an extensive collection of genre lit (westerns, romances, mysteries …)? So maybe they *are* (also) entertainment centres, indoor parks, if you will. But then where or where is the quiet place? Are there no quiet public spaces left??

What's wrong with selling your organs?

It seems to be morally acceptable to sell one's blood, sperm, eggs, and hair. So what's so unacceptable about selling one's kidney, for example?

And in case people think the forementioned sales are unacceptable, let me make another analogy: it's okay to get paid to play football – why is using your body as a linebacker in order to earn an income acceptable, but using it as an organ store is not?

Is it because the person offering a kidney is doing so due to economic duress? So may be the linebacker. In fact, all of us who *have* to work, to pay for food and shelter, offer our bodies (brains included, sometimes) under economic duress to do so.

Is it that the linebacker is making an offer of service, but the organ seller is making an offer of product? The former is temporary, the latter permanent? But many people, not just athletes, suffer permanent debilitating injury.

Of course, there's a possibility that people will start taking other people's physical resources without consent. But theft and slavery are nothing new.

Will it lead to a black market? More often, legalizing something leads to regulation and a diminishment of black market activity.

Actually, we don't sell blood. Not here in Canada. We give it away. Is it because it's so necessary? Is *that* the difference? One can live without football ... So is it that organs *for sale* violates the presumed equal right to life? But then all the pharmaceuticals and surgeries required to live with an otherwise fatal condition should be free. And food.

Assisted Suicide and Unassisted Suicide: What's the Difference?

Discussions about whether or not to legalize assisted suicide often fail to take into account the fact that *un*assisted suicide [1] is already legal in many countries. Failure to consider this fact means that unless there is a significant difference between assisted suicide and unassisted suicide that justifies prohibiting the former while permitting the latter, one must either accept inconsistency or reconsider. [2]

There are six reasons typically given for prohibiting assisted suicide: the tragic death; preferred alternatives; the social good; upstaging God; the slippery slope; the possibility of abuse. I argue that these reasons are equally applicable to unassisted suicide; therefore, again, one must either accept inconsistency or argue on the same grounds for prohibiting unassisted suicide.

1. The Tragic Death. Some argue against legalizing assisted suicide on the grounds that people will die tragically, acting on a decision made in a despairing moment. But this is as true (perhaps *more* true for one doesn't have to go through the process of obtaining assistance) for unassisted suicide. The consequent death may also be tragic – premature, avoidable, and/or perhaps even the regrettable result of a bad decision.

2. Preferred Alternatives. Others argue against legalizing assisted suicide on the grounds that the better solution is to improve the standard of care for the terminally ill and the severely disabled so they won't want to choose death; counselling is another often-mentioned preferred alternative to assisted suicide. But again, this is as true for unassisted suicide: there are alternatives, such as psychological or philosophical counselling, or even, if applicable, employment, that may be preferable to suicide.

3. The Social Good. There are many variants of this argument,

but all conclude that assisted suicide is not to be legalized on the grounds that some social good transcends personal autonomy. Some claim that no one should have the right to unilaterally make a decision that will affect others: "We are individuals living in a society, a community, and the community has rights when it comes to an individual member's behaviour. Our whole society is based on this, and one person's actions can set off emotions or consequences for his family and his immediate neighbours in the community" (Senate of Canada, Dionne, p.56). Making a slightly different case, some claim that legalizing assisted suicide contradicts the social value of respect for life and on that basis argue for prohibiting assisted suicide: "Euthanasia and assisted suicide are contrary to the basic respect for human life which is at the core of societal values" (Senate of Canada, McGregor, p.55). But again, advocates of some social good seem to have forgotten that by allowing unassisted suicide, we already allow personal autonomy to override the social good, however it may be defined.

4. Upstaging God. Arguments to prohibit assisted suicide on the grounds that only God gives life, so only God can take it away (see, for example, J. V. Sullivan) are equally relevant to unassisted suicide: whether the suicide is assisted or not, death occurs by a human hand, not by a god's hand. Therefore, proponents of such arguments must go on to argue for the prohibition of unassisted suicide (which, admittedly, they often do) or accept inconsistency.

5. The Slippery Slope. Assisted suicide is often argued against because of the fear that allowing unassisted suicide will lead to the acceptability, or at least the (increasing) occurrence, of involuntary euthanasia. However, there are relatively clear lines on the slope that can prevent us from slipping, notably, the presence of consent.

6. The Possibility of Abuse. Not withstanding the forementioned

relatively clear lines, it is possible that allowing assisted suicide will lead to abuses. But this is true of most activities subject to legislation; consider, for example, driving while intoxicated.

There are, however, two distinctions between assisted suicide and unassisted suicide that may justify illegalizing the one while legalizing the other: assistance and voluntariness. However, in both cases, I find the difference too weak, too problematic, or simply too questionable, to support legal differentiation.

(1) Assistance. At first glance, it seems that assisted suicide requires the assistance of another person while unassisted suicide does not, and perhaps it is this difference that justifies prohibiting the one while permitting the other.

However, depending on the method used for the unassisted suicide, *the difference of assistance is often merely a matter of degree*. For example, the person who uses an overdose of sleeping pills or morphine needs someone to provide those sleeping pills or that morphine. The same applies to the gun, the razor blade, and so on. Perhaps the only *true* unassisted suicide would be something like jumping off a cliff or swimming out to sea.

This matter of degree can be present in three respects.

(a) Immediacy. In the case of assisted suicide, the means are usually provided at the moment, whereas in the case of unassisted suicide, the means are perhaps more typically provided somewhat before the moment. But, in the case of unassisted suicide, they may also be provided within minutes of the moment: the drugstore salesperson who sells me the sleeping pills may be a five-minute walk from my apartment, and I may make the purchase, come home, and suicide right away.

While this difference in immediacy *is* a difference, it is an unclear difference, a fuzzy line difference, and therefore not, I think, strong enough to support a legal distinction between assisted suicide and unassisted suicide. Would we say that provision of the means for suicide within twenty-four hours of the death counts as an assisted suicide, but provision of the means within twenty-five hours does not?

(b) Directness. Perhaps it is the directness of the assistance that makes the significant difference: after all, feeding the pills to a person until s/he dies is a lot different than simply putting them on a store shelf.

Yes, but again, this difference can reduce to a very small and surely insignificant difference: putting them on the shelf, putting them on the counter, putting them in a person's mailbox, putting them in a person's hand, putting them on a person's tongue – where one draws a line is not that clear. Certainly it is not clear enough to support the weight of criminal difference. [2]

(c) Awareness. Perhaps a stronger difference between the assistance provided for assisted suicide and that provided for unassisted suicide concerns the awareness of the provider: for example, in the case of assisted suicide, the person who provides the pills *knows* they are for the purpose of suicide, but in the case of unassisted suicide, the drugstore salesperson reasonably assumes they're for the purpose of a good night's sleep.

But how can this difference be significant? Why should it matter whether or not the pill provider is aware of the purpose for which the pills are to be used? Knowingly assisting is a greater degree of assistance, yes, but typically, such foreknowledge is a problem only when the intended purpose is illegal; in such cases, the provider is guilty of conspiring to commit whatever it is that is about to be committed. But committing suicide is as legal as getting a good night's sleep. Conspiring to commit suicide, then, should be as unproblematic as 'conspiring' to 'commit' such a good night's sleep. *Assisting* a suicide should be as legal as a suicide.

Furthermore, since it is *physical* assistance we're talking about, this element gives a sort of supremacy to the body over the mind: it doesn't matter what the mind wills – if the body *can* (and doesn't require assistance), it's legal, but if the body *can't*, it's illegal. This seems to be inconsistent with current social attitudes: we seem to value the mind more than the body ('It doesn't matter what you look like, it's what's inside that counts'). It also contradicts legal principles that excuse actions of the body when the mind wasn't willing: if one is forced to *do* something against one's *will*, it doesn't 'count'. Even death itself is determined by the state of the brain rather than the state of the heart or lungs: one is pronounced dead when one is 'brain dead' – until that time, one can be kept alive with pacemakers and respirators.

On the other hand, illegalizing assisted suicide (and not unassisted suicide) because of the physical assistance may not so much be a nod to the supremacy of the physical, but a nod to the possibility of coercion. Because of the *assistance*, assisted suicide may be understood to be less voluntary than unassisted suicide After all, although one can choose to swallow or not, one has no voluntary control over one's veins – one can't choose to accept or not the morphine that is injected into one's arm.

(2) Voluntariness. Voluntariness is the second distinction between assisted suicide and unassisted suicide that may justify the legal difference. To assume that physical

assistance increases the likelihood of coercion or, conversely, that lack of physical assistance decreases the likelihood of coercion is to assume a very shallow definition of coercion. For one thing, coercion need not be immediate or direct: suppose someone said to you a day, a week, or a month earlier, that if you didn't kill yourself, he would kill your children; surely your consequent unassisted suicide could not be considered fully voluntary. It is more difficult to determine the will of the mind than the act of the body (the latter is subject to simple observation), and we are naïve to assume that what we see is all there is to it, that the body is indeed acting according to the mind's will, that the mind has not been somehow coerced.

It is not unsurprising, therefore, that there are many analyses of consent and coercion that indicate not only that assisted suicide should be as legal as unassisted suicide, but that it should, perhaps, be *more* legal: with assisted suicide, we can be *more*, not *less*, certain that consent is present and coercion absent. For example, a survey of the medical ethics literature suggests that valid consent is capable (referring to the capacity to understand and so form a judgement), informed (regarding one's condition, the proposed action, its risks, consequences, and alternatives), and voluntary (that is, freely willed by the self). The presence of a third party, as is the case with assisted suicide and not unassisted suicide, can come closer to guaranteeing that all three conditions are met.

With respect to the first condition, a third party can subject the person to a test of mental competence to be sure that the capability condition is met. [3]

With respect to the second condition, the third party can provide the person with information, in writing and orally, once or on several occasions, to be sure that she or he understands not only the proposed course of action (the suicide), but also the alternatives, as well as the consequences (to others). The presence of a third party can also help ensure that the decision is not a tragic, 'bad' decision, but rather one in which respect for life and even sanctity of life is preserved.

The third condition, voluntariness, is difficult to determine, depending as it does on free will. I will assume that we do indeed have free will. I will further propose that, barring coercion, the condition of voluntariness is dependent on the forementioned conditions of capability and informedness. That is, if the person *is* capable *and* informed, and coercion is not present, we can assume that his or her action, whether it is the commission of suicide or the expression of the request for assistance to suicide, is indeed voluntary.

But how do we establish whether or not coercion is present? *External* coercion, usually thought to refer to physical force applied by one person to another causing the other to do something, is relatively easy to establish. *Internal* coercion, on the other hand, usually referring to one's mental states – fears, desires, beliefs, attitudes – is harder to determine. Indeed, a difficult question is 'When do our internal states merely *cause* our behaviour and when do they *coerce* it?'

Johnson [4] notes that in a sense all of our actions are more or less coerced by the reasons for them, but this is not a useful definition of 'coercion' as it would render *all* consent invalid.

Katz [5] presents as broad a perspective: when he specifies voluntariness as a condition of consent, he goes on to say that "any informed consent doctrine, to be realistic, must take into account the biological, psychological, intellectual, and social constraints imposed upon thought and action". Of course, one's neurochemicals can affect one's clarity of thought which in turn affects one's beliefs which in turn affect one's attitudes – which are also affected by the society in which one lives. The lines demarcating regions of control of self by self become fuzzy indeed.

One solution is to adopt Cohen's distinction [6] between (i) narrow or tight coercion, in which case there is a deliberate effort by someone to pressure another to do something, which makes consent invalid by making it involuntary, and (ii) general or loose coercion, in which case one is pressured by the general conditions one finds oneself in or by the desires and needs one has, which does *not* invalidate consent. Such a distinction would invalidate the request for assistance made by the disabled person who is being encouraged by next of kin who cannot afford to care for him/her anymore, but it would not invalidate the request made by that same person simply because of the circumstance of disability he/she finds him/herself in. Establishing 'deliberateness' and 'pressure' would not be easy, however; the troubling distinction between 'explicit' and 'implicit' would surely arise.

Perhaps considering both consent and coercion to be matters of degree is the best we can do. So even though we may not be able to establish with certainty whether or not the desire for suicide was voluntary, surely we can establish this with *greater* certainty in the case of assisted suicide, when there are other people involved to validate or confirm the desire. At the very least, we can require a sort of superior suicide note: we could require, for example, that on three separate occasions, in the presence of three completely separate and disinterested sets of people – to include medical, police, legal, and governmental representatives – the person freely and fully expressed consent, to be documented with audiotape, videotape, and signed transcript. [7]

To summarize, not one of the six standard arguments, nor the distinction of assistance, nor the distinction of voluntariness, is sufficient to support a difference between assisted suicide and unassisted suicide with regard to their legal status. (Or, I might add, with regard to their moral status.)

---

1. I consider *unassisted suicide* to be the regular kind of suicide involving one person, the person who ends his/her life, by actions solely performed by him/herself. I consider *assisted suicide* to describe a situation in which a person wants to commit suicide, but is physically unable to carry out his/her own wishes and so must ask another to perform the necessary actions; in much of the literature, this is referred to as *voluntary euthanasia*.

However, *voluntary euthanasia* is often used to further include situations in which a person wants to commit suicide, *is* physically able to do so, but nevertheless asks for the assistance of another – whether out of ignorance, cowardice, a desire to ensure that the action is successful, or a desire to ensure a certain kind of suicide. I do not consider this situation, but note the importance of accessibility to effective and painless methods that are user-friendly, even for the feeble or disabled.

Non-voluntary euthanasia is often used to describe situations in which the wishes of the person are not known for sure, but the 'proxy consent' of another is considered satisfactory justification for a third party to end the life of that person.

Lastly, *involuntary euthanasia* is often used to describe situations in which it is known that the person does *not* wish his/her life to end, and yet another acts to achieve that result. Like many others, I consider this to be indistinguishable from *murder* and do not consider it at all.

2. The distinction between passive and active might be considered here, the idea being that withholding food, for example, is different than providing an injection, the former being passive, *not* considered an instance of assisted suicide. However, first, the passive, an act of omission, can still assist – it's just a very indirect form of assistance. Second, the distinction is merely semantic, a matter of description: for example, when I don't shake your hand (passive, an act of omission), I am holding my hand at my side (active, an act of commission). Third, the distinction presumes a supremacy, a priority, a sort of 'right-of-way' to 'the course of nature' (fate, God, whatever) such that an act that 'interferes' is the one considered active; this supremacy is indefensible.

3. A reminder may be in order at this point that I define assisted suicide to exclude what many refer to as non-voluntary euthanasia, cases in which the person is unconscious, comatose, infantile, or otherwise unable to actually request assistance. I believe it is possible, however, to argue for proxy consent; indeed, I suggest that valid proxy consent is what distinguishes euthanasia from murder.

As one might guess, proxy consent is even more slippery than consent. But that has not been, in our legal past, sufficient reason to disallow actions based on proxy consent: parent guardians give consent on behalf of their young children all the time; significant others give consent on behalf of unconscious adults.

The first important question is 'When is proxy consent required?' That is, in which cases do we say consent by the individual concerned is inadmissible and/or impossible? I think we can simply apply the criteria of valid consent under discussion: if the person is capable, informed, and voluntary, then proxy consent is unnecessary.

At the extremes, application of this test will be easy: an unconscious or comatose person is clearly incapable of giving/withholding consent; we're also pretty sure about infants and severely retarded people; the line gets fuzzy with older children and moderately retarded people. Perhaps a test of mental competence would keep the line clear – but it had better be a very good test.

The second important question has to be 'What constitutes valid proxy consent?' Certainly it must have the attributes of valid direct consent: it must be capable, informed, and voluntary. Additionally, well, there are a few possibilities. One is to apply the 'reasonable standard' criterion and say that the decision must be what any reasonable person would make. But what is 'reasonable' and who decides?

Another is to say that the decision must be in the best interests of the individual concerned. But this has problems similar to the reasonable standard solution – what is 'best' and who decides?

A third possibility is to say that the decision must be what that individual would make if s/he were able (if s/he were capable, informed, and voluntary). This depends on guesswork, unless a living will exists – though a living will essentially changes euthanasia to assisted suicide.

A fourth possibility might be that since personal autonomy is clearly impossible, a decision should be made on the basis of social utility: why should at least three people sacrifice their lives to save one person? Is that one person worth three? (Round the clock care equals three eight-hour shifts, hence three people. However, since that just accounts for labour and not for food, shelter, and the specialized technology usually required, the 'people equivalent' figure would probably be greater than that.)

Lastly, we could decide on the basis of actual and/or potential quality of life – not its value to others, but its value to the individual. This may translate into specific criteria such as the presence of continual (?) severe (?) pain and/or (?) chance of recovery.

4. Johnson, Deborah G. "Prisoners and Consent to Experimentation." Consent: Concept, Capacity, Conditions, and Constraints. Ed. L. T. Sargent. Wiesbaden: Franz Steiner Verlag GMBH, 1979. 167-179.

5. Katz, Jay. "Informed Consent in the Therapeutic Relationship: Law and Ethics." Biomedical ethics. Eds. T. A. Mappes and J. S. Zembaty. New York: McGraw-Hill Book Company, 1986. 94-103.

6. Presented in Turkington, Richard C. "The Role of Institutional Coercion to Full or Informal Consent to Medical Experiments in Prisons." Consent: Concept, Capacity, Conditions, and Constraints. Ed. L. T. Sargent. Wiesbaden: Franz Steiner Verlag GMBH, 1979. 193-200.

7. Such a requirement would have the additional advantage of going a long way toward distinguishing between assisted suicide and murder.

Rising Above Natural Selection

We need to rise above natural selection. Otherwise, as a species, we will continue to become dumb and dumber.

Who has the family of five? Not the physicist or philosopher. She's chosen not to have any kids. And not the biologist or sociologist. He stopped at two.

And who's having the family of ten? The people in 'developing' countries who either don't have access to contraception, let alone a grade twelve education, or who subscribe to some indefensible religio-cultural belief about family.

How do we rise above natural selection? That's the question no one wants to ask. Because the answer is so clear. And so awful.

But not nearly as awful as a species of idiots.

The Inconsistency of Not Requiring Parents to be Licensed

The proposal to license parents – that is, to require people to obtain a license, by demonstrating certain attributes and/or abilities, before they produce and possibly rear children – is usually rejected, usually quickly and loudly. I contend that this rejection reveals inconsistent thinking, to the extent that certain other regulations already in place are accepted.

First, let's consider cloning, assisted insemination by donor (AID), in vitro fertilization (IVF), and surrogacy, all of which deal with the production part of being a parent. Anticipating that at some point in the near future, we will be able to clone human beings, one might also reasonably anticipate that such cloning will not be unregulated. For example, I doubt we'll allow someone to create his own private workforce or his own little army. And I suspect we'll prohibit cloning oneself for mere ego gratification. Doing it just because it's fun will certainly be illegal (and I expect it won't even be imaginable to do it "without really thinking about it," let alone "by accident"). I suspect we'll enforce some sort of quality control, such that cloned human beings shall not exist in pain or be severely "compromised" with respect to basic functioning. Actually, I suspect one will have to apply for a license and satisfy rigorous screening standards, and I assume this will include the submission, and approval, of a detailed plan regarding responsibility for the cloned human being – surely we won't allow a scientist to create it and then just leave it on the lab's doorstep one night when he leaves. And yet we accept all of these motives and behaviours when life is created in backseats and bedrooms.

In fact, the National Bioethics Advisory Commission [1] has already recommended "regulating" cloning, to the point of outright prohibition, and it has done so because of the physical and psychological harms that may result, the "severe developmental abnormalities" (p.48) and the negative effects on the child's self-worth and "experience of freedom" (p.51). Are we not concerned about such physical and psychological harms when they may result from coital reproduction?

In our more immediate present, parenting is also regulated when it involves access to new reproductive technologies (NRTs), such as AID and IVF. The Canadian Royal Commission on New Reproductive Technologies [2] requires, for example, that all potential sperm donors provide detailed information about their health and the health of their first-degree relatives; this information is to be reviewed by a clinical geneticist and "any indication of serious genetic anomalies or other high-risk factors" is to be grounds for disqualification (p.476). They also require donors to take tests for HIV and other infectious diseases (p.476). It is perplexing that these requirements apply only when sperm is to be used by someone *other* than the sperm producer's "partner" (p.476).

Furthermore, the Commission recommends that "a license [be] required to perform insemination at any site other than the vagina even if the recipient is the social partner" (p.484). Why, when the vagina is the site, is it "anything goes", but otherwise, we "proceed with care"?

The Commission also recommends that the woman seeking to become impregnated through various assistive NRTs sign a statement indicating that she has "received, read, and understood" not only information outlining "the risks, responsibilities, and implications of donor insemination ... " (p.481), but also the sperm screening and medical test results (p.476). Why shouldn't women be required to provide such informed consent for "unassisted" reproduction as well?

Counselling should also to be provided, the Commission

goes on to say, that addresses "information about alternatives … such as … living without children; avoidance of exposure to risk factors … ; [and] some exploration of questions related to values and goals that patients may wish to take into account when making their decisions … ." (p.571). Again, why shouldn't we also require this of those intending to "access" "old reproductive technologies"?

Regulations concerning "surrogacy" reveal a similar double standard. Susan Ince [3] describes the various tests one needs to pass before being accepted for a gestational contract: a thorough medical exam, genetic screening if indicated, intelligence testing, and psychological evaluation. She also describes the "extensive behavioral controls over the surrogate" which include prohibitions on smoking, drinking, and illegal drugs, as well as mandatory medical, psychological, and counselling appointments (p.105); "any action," she says, "that 'can be deemed to be dangerous to the well-being of the unborn child' constitutes a breach of contract" (p.106). Why should children born of surrogates be privileged to a higher standard of care in their creation than children not so born?

Lori Andrews [4] has pointed out that "surrogacy contracts contain lengthy riders detailing the myriad risks of pregnancy, so potential surrogates are much better informed on that topic than are most women who get pregnant in a more traditional fashion" (p.172). Why do we not require this of *all* those who intend to gestate?

Next, let's consider custody, fostering, and adoption, all of which deal with the rearing part of being a parent. When a married-with-kids couple separates, the parents usually try to demonstrate to the court their parental competence in the hope of being granted custody of the children. Such competence is taken to include their knowledge of child-rearing, various personal qualities such as patience and sensitivity, their availability to the children, and so on. As long as they do not separate, however, such competence is apparently irrelevant – they are granted custody of the children, whatever their level of knowledge, skills, and commitment.

People who want to foster or adopt children must undergo similar "tests of competence," including a home visit and a background check. Roger McIntire [5] pointedly asks what would happen if this were not so, if adoption agencies used instead a first-come, first-served basis: "Imagine some drunk stumbling up and saying 'I'll take that cute little blond-haired girl over there'" (p.133). And yet that's pretty much what we currently allow with regard to non-adoptive parenting. Why do we cling to the irrational belief that biological parents are *necessarily* competent parents – in the face of overwhelming evidence to the contrary? Indeed, as Elizabeth Bartholet [6] asks, "Why would anyone think that those who consciously plan to adopt someone else's child pose *more* of a risk than those who fall unwittingly into pregnancy?" (p.69, emphasis added).

Daycare workers and teachers – people to whom we entrust the care and nurturing of children for up to 8 hours a day – must be licensed. They must actually study full-time for months, if not years, and pass several examinations before the state allows them that responsibility. And yet someone can be responsible not only for a child's education, but for virtually everything about the child, for twenty-four hours a day until that child is six years of age – that is, for the duration of the critical, formative years – and he or she doesn't even have to so much as read a pamphlet about child development. Why not?

Why *are* we are so inconsistent – why *don't* we license parents when parenthood occurs as a consequence of sexual intercourse? Perhaps it's because we don't take parenting seriously. And yet we *do* take it seriously when it occurs *apart* from sexual intercourse, when NRTs and foster arrangements are involved.

Perhaps, as Jack Westman [7] claims, it is because parenting doesn't have any economic value in our society (p.3). Surrogates and foster parents *are* paid, so perhaps it's that regulation is warranted when money is involved. However, not only does this explanation suggest we're more concerned about our money than our children, it doesn't account for our evaluations of competence when co-parents divorce (and not, for example, when they marry).

Perhaps we don't license parenting because it's considered a *private* matter. When parenting involves NRTs and fostering, however, it fails to be private – perhaps *that's* the element that warrants regulation. But it's unclear why the involvement of others should have that effect. Further, perhaps the more important point is not whether parenting *is* private, but whether it *should be* private; we used to think one spouse hitting another was a private matter, but, fortunately, we have changed our minds and now consider state involvement, including regulation, to be warranted in such cases.

Or perhaps the difference is that children are considered to be the private *property* of their parents. However, given the time, effort, and resources involved, children produced through NRTs would be even *more* so the private property of their creators – and yet there we have regulation. More importantly, especially since the anti-slavery movement, we have established good grounds for rejecting the notion of people as property.

One last possible explanation for our inconsistency is that we have a *right* to have children, and regulation would interfere with that right. But then don't the scientists cloning embryos in their labs have a right to have those children? What about the women seeking AID and IVF? What about the men seeking surrogates? What about the people wanting to adopt? If we have a right to have children, and if regulation interferes with that right, then regulation in those cases should be rejected. To be consistent, one would have to modify the rights claim to say something like 'We have a right to engage in reproductive sexual intercourse and to rear the results.'

But on what grounds can we claim this right? Merely *having* a capability does not entail the *right to exercise* that capability. Some argue that the right to reproduce is a natural right (see S. L. Floyd and D. Pomerantz for a critique of this view), some refer to its importance to personal well-being and identity (see Dan Brock and John A. Robertson), and some point to the need or desire to have a child (see Chadwick for a critique of this view). But whatever the nature or justification for the right to "have children," rights are seldom considered absolute: they may be overidden by competing rights – the rights of another individual or the rights of society.

So we come back to the question of whether there are relevant and significant differences between, on the one hand, parentage involving NRTs and parenting involving fostering, and on the other hand, parentage and parenting involving sexual intercourse – differences that warrant regulation on the one hand but not on the other. One possibility is that NRTs and arrangements in which the children one nurtures are not one's own biological issue are unnatural. But the biological material is natural – why does it matter which cells are involved or how they get into a uterus? Furthermore, it's unclear why 'unnatural' should imply 'subject to greater regulation.'

Another possibility is that with NRTs and the other arrangements, people are asking for society's help, they are asking for the use of societal resources – and that's why permission is required: not only to *use* those resources, but to ensure they're not *mis*used. But people reproducing without NRT assistance *also* use societal resources, most notably through the healthcare system for prenatal, natal, and postnatal care.

Furthermore, in both cases, the resulting child certainly uses societal resources.

So it would seem there are no relevant and significant differences. There is, however, one relevant and significant *similarity:* the potential for serious harm to those who have a right to be free from such harm. Parentage, however it occurs, involves the creation of a life, a life that is sensitive to the various harms and goods that its creators can bring about. This power alone entails responsibility, by the individual and by the state (to ensure the individual meets that responsibility).

And parenting, however it occurs, involves the development of a person who will interact with the rest of the world, taking and giving, for good and for bad. So whether framed as a consequentialist argument or as a rights argument, I contend that the consideration of harm is sufficient grounds for at least some sort of parent licensing program [8].

Of course, consistency, wouldn't be the only benefit of licensing parents. As Joseph Fletcher [9] says, "It is depressing, not comforting, to realize that most people are accidents" (p.36). And insofar as intended children are more apt than unintended children to receive love and adequate care, licensing, by requiring intentional action prior to birth (application, at least, and perhaps also the acquisition of certain capacities and competencies), could increase the odds that children are indeed loved and cared for. As Margaret Battin [10] suggests, licensing would have the same effect as mandatory contraception: "Our ways of thinking about pregnancy and childbearing would undergo radical change – from something one accepts or rejects when it happens to something one chooses to begin" (p.30).

Another benefit, insofar as a licensing program would include an educational component, is described by Philip Kitcher [11] (who proposes education *instead* of licensing, not *as part of* licensing): "People would make ... *right* decisions because they would understand the consequences of their decisions, both for their offspring and for society" (p.202, emphasis added). (Although we'd like to believe there is a connection between education and ethics, perhaps this would apply only some of the time to some of the people.)

Yet another benefit of licensing parents is that which Gregory Kavka [12] identifies as a benefit of genetic engineering but which could apply to paren*ting* as well as paren*tage*: "We might come to view parents as being more responsible for how their children turn out than we now view them" (p.172-3). Kavka goes on to describe this responsibility almost existentially, as "awesome, possibly overwhelming" (p.173) – perhaps that response to parenthood is overdue.

---

1. National Bioethics Advisory Commission, "Cloning Human Beings" in *Flesh of My Flesh: The Ethics of Cloning Humans*. ed. Gregory E. Pence (Lanham, MD: Rowman & Littlefield, 1998).
2. Royal Commission on New Reproductive Technologies, *Proceed with Care* (Ottawa, ON: Minister of Government Services Canada, 1993).
3. Susan Ince, "Inside the Surrogate Industry" in *Test-Tube Women*. eds. Rita Arditti, Renate Duelli Klein, and Shelley Minden. (London, UK: Pandora Press, 1984).
4. Lori B. Andrews, *New Conceptions: A Consumer's Guide to the Newest Infertility Treatments* (New York: Ballantyne Books, 1985).
5. Roger McIntire, "Parenthood Training or Mandatory Birth Control: Take Your Choice," *Psychology Today* (October 1973).
6. Elizabeth Bartholet, *Family Bonds* (Boston: Houghton Mifflin, 1993).
7. Jack C. Westman, Licensing Parents: Can We Prevent Child Abuse and Neglect? (New York: Plenum Press, 1994).
8. True, a license would restrict rights *before* harm is done (that is, *in order to prevent* harm), rather than *because* harm has been done, so to some extent the proposal to license parents suggests the presumption of guilt rather than innocence. However, restricting one's rights need not be perceived as punishment for some as yet undemonstrated wrongdoing. Furthermore, the same preventive rationale is used for issuing other sorts of licenses, such as drivers' licenses.
9. Joseph Fletcher, *The Ethics of Genetic Control: Ending Reproductive Roulette* (Buffalo, NY: Prometheus Books, 1988).
10. Margaret P. Battin, "Sex & Consequences: World Population Growth vs. Reproductive Rights," *Philosophic Exchange* 27 (1997).

11. Philip Kitcher, *The Lives to Come* (NY: Simon & Schuster), 1996).
12. Gregory S. Kavka, "Upside Risks: Social Consequences of Beneficial Biotechnology" in *Are Genes Us? The Social Consequences of the New Genetics*. ed. Carl F. Cranor (New Brunswick, NJ: Rutgers University Press, 1994).

Legislating Prenatal Care

Prenatal abuse may not be new; after all, tobacco and alcohol have been around for a long time. Our awareness of it is relatively new, however: perhaps because the tendrils of our social system have lengthened; perhaps because medical technology has made it more possible to keep debilitated newborns alive. In any case, legislating prenatal care has become an important issue. And perhaps this is especially so because of increases in both the use of illegal drugs (which can *cause* harm) and the availability of fetal therapies (which can *prevent* harm).

Use during pregnancy of illegal drugs (such as crack cocaine and heroin) as well as legal drugs (such as alcohol and nicotine) can cause, in the newborn, excruciating pain, vomiting, inability to sleep, reluctance to feed, diarrhea leading to shock and death, severe anaemia, growth retardation, mental retardation, central nervous system abnormalities, and malformations of the kidneys, intestines, head and spinal cord [1, 2, 3]. Refusal of fetal therapy techniques (such as surgery, blood infusions, and vitamin regimens) can result in respiratory distress, and various genetic disorders and defects such as spina bifida and hydrocephalus [2].

One task is to sort out the difference, if any, between legally insisting that a pregnant woman *not* do X (e.g., drink alcohol) and legally insisting that she *do* X (e.g., take certain vitamin supplements). Rachels [4], examining the similar passive/active distinction in euthanasia, argues that because the intent (relieving suffering) and consequence (death) are the same, there is no moral difference. So too with prenatal care: because the intent (producing a healthy newborn) and the consequence (a healthy newborn) are the same, there is no moral difference between legislation that *prohibits* X and legislation that *requires* X.

However, there is not necessarily a relationship between

morality and legality. Canada and the U.S., unlike several European countries [5] does not have 'Good Samaritan' laws: we are legally bound, generally speaking, not to harm others, but we are *not* legally bound to *help* them. Therefore, as far as consistency is concerned, one can more easily justify legislation against abuse than legislation in favour of care. However, this may simply make us consistent with an already poor situation – perhaps Canada *should* have 'Good Samaritan' laws.

This does, however, lead us to the crucial question 'When does lack of help become harm?' – 'When does lack of care become abuse?' If we could establish an acceptable baseline, perhaps we could say that action less than that is illegal, more than that is optional. Such is the case with child abuse: beating a child is illegal, but allowing it to watch four hours of violent television programming every day is not. (Go figure.) Accordingly, one could argue that personal sacrifice should not be legally required in this case when minimal decency is all the law requires in other cases [6]. The woman should not be required to do *all* that is in the *best* interests of the zygote/embryo/fetus, but only what's 'reasonable', conforming to what Mathieu (p. 43) refers to as a 'minimum needs' standard [7].

Another approach would be a sort of 'cost benefit' analysis. For example, giving up alcohol is little to ask to ensure a newborn free of mental retardation [8], but giving up one's job may be too much to ask to ensure the newborn is not a little premature.

Before we define what legislation is *reasonable*, however, we have to establish the right of the state to legislate in this case in the first place. How can we say on the one hand 'This is my body and you have no right to deny me an abortion' and on the other hand 'You *can* tell me what to drink and what not to drink when I'm pregnant'. To state the contradiction in other terms, how can we say prenatal abuse is a crime, is harming a person, but abortion is *not* a crime, is not killing a person. Obviously, one can't have it both ways: either women do or do not have the right to control their own bodies; either the fetus is or is not a person.

However, permitting abortion while prohibiting prenatal harm need not be contradictory. One, there are grounds other than the right to control one's body that justify abortion; for example, abortion could be permitted because the fetus is not an actual person. Even if it *is* a person, abortion may be permissible: it is sometimes acceptable to kill persons, most notably in cases of self-defence. Furthermore, there are other kinds of rights, dependent or not upon the personhood of the fetus, that can be invoked to support abortion (see Thomson and English).

And prenatal harm can be prohibited even if one does have the right to control one's body; after all, non-pregnant people presumably with the right to control their bodies are not permitted to cause *post*natal harm. And personhood again may be irrelevant: the fetus may *not* be a person and still it may be *un*acceptable to cause it harm; the arguments of animal rights advocates such as Regan and Singer may be applicable in this case.

Two, one can argue for a continuum of rights. The right to control one's own body is not an 'all or nothing' right: not everything one does with one's body is legal or morally acceptable. For example, it's generally illegal for people to use their bodies to break other people's legs. With respect to the contradiction in personhood terms, well, in our society, not all persons have the same, or even equal, rights. An institutionalized person (whether in a hospital or a prison) doesn't have the same rights as an non-institutionalized person. More relevantly, a two-year old infant doesn't have the same rights as a twenty-year old adult. As Callahan and Knight [9] and Mathieu point out, many rights are attached to age in a rather arbitrary fashion because the development of abilities is continuous rather than discrete. So while a fifteen-and-three-quarters-year old might argue that she is just as mature as her sixteen-year old friend and therefore should have just as much a right to get a beginner drivers' licence, a six-year old could not make the same argument.

With similar arbitrariness – and with similar justification because the continuousness of development *demands* such arbitrariness – we could argue that an eight-month old fetus person doesn't have the same rights as a one-month old infant person, and that a one-week old zygote person doesn't have the same rights as the eight-month old fetus person.

The two important rights that concern us here, the right to life (or the right not to be killed) and the right not to be harmed, can be placed on the continuum such that, for example, only old fetus persons (and not young fetus persons, embryo persons, or zygote persons) have both the right to life and the right not to be harmed. Or we could say that all persons have the right not to be harmed but only fetus persons have the right to life. Thus one could condone (certain) abortion *and* condemn (certain) prenatal harm without contradiction (depending on where the lines are drawn).

Three, one can argue for a continuum of body: while the woman does have the right to control her body, what is considered 'her body' changes through the pregnancy parallel to the changes in the personhood of the zygote/embryo/ fetus: the less it is a person, the more it is her body; the more it is a person, the less it is her body. Likewise, one can argue for a continuum of personhood: rather than assuming that the zygote/embryo/fetus is or is not a person, as if personhood is an 'all or nothing' attribute, it may be more reasonable, more reflective of our reality, to consider the many possible criteria – human genetic material, brainwaves, heartbeat, quickening, sentience, viability, social visibility, ability to communicate, self-motivated activity, capacity for rational thought, consciousness, interests of one's own, etc. – and establish some sort of continuum of personhood. One can then 'assign' fewer rights to 'lesser persons'. The acceptability of aborting a being with minimal personhood would not then contradict the unacceptability of harming a being with considerably more personhood.

Four, one can distinguish between the potentially born and the preborn according to the woman's intent. A little background is in order for this solution. The notion of 'potential person' figures prominently in the discussion about abortion. To some, it is the fact that a fetus is a potential person that justifies an anti-abortion stance. To others, potential persons have only potential rights [10]. And the notion of 'future persons' is prominent in environmental ethics (though discussion tends toward 'duties toward' rather than 'rights of').

Adding the notions of 'actual persons' and 'conventional persons', Callahan and Knight make the following four-tiered distinction. *Actual persons* are human beings with those characteristics such as "a concept of oneself as an ongoing being with at least some kinds of plans and stakes" (p. 145) that compel us to recognize strong moral rights; full emergence of these characteristics occurs long after birth. *Conventional persons* are human beings that are not yet actual persons but that have been born. "A prenatal human being is a *potential person* when it is the case that (1) it has the capacities to develop the kinds of characteristics that are relevant to compelling a recognition of a being as an actual person and (2) if its life were supported, it would be born, gaining conventional entry into the set of persons at birth" (p. 152, my italics). Lastly, "a prenatal human being is a *future person* if (1) it is a potential person and (2) it will, in fact, gain conventional entry into the class of persons through birth" (p. 152, my italics).

I accept Callahan and Knight's definitions of a potential person and a future person, but I want to emphasize, indeed *specify*, that it is the woman who decides whether or not a prenatal human being will, in fact, 'gain such entry'. That is to say, the single determinant differentiating between potential persons and future persons is the woman's intent: *if she intends to carry the being to term and give it birth, then it shall be deemed a future person; if she does not intend to carry it to term and give it birth, it shall be deemed a potential person.* To underscore birth as the difference, and to eliminate the impression that a potential person is indeed some kind of *person*, I will henceforth refer to potential persons and future persons as, respectively, the 'potentially born' and the 'preborn'.

One can then argue that a woman has full/usual rights over her body when the potentially born are involved, but she has restricted rights when the preborn are involved. Her intent to carry the zygote/embryo/fetus to term and give it birth constitutes consent and entails a forfeiture of certain rights. The extent of forfeit or the nature of restrictions can be worked out according to the cost benefit strategy mentioned previously. Or, one can assign rights to the potentially born and the preborn such that permitting abortion and prohibiting prenatal harm are not contradictory.

One could also argue that the woman's intent that the potentially born be born (i.e., be a preborn) constitutes a promise and that this promise is the basis for its right not to be harmed or killed – or at least for moral obligations on her part both not to harm it and to provide it with the life she has promised [11].

Another approach is to argue that unlike a potentially born, a preborn does have a future – it does have interests that can be jeopardized. This may be further grounds for granting it the right not to be harmed, or more specifically, the right to begin life with a sound mind and body. If it's illegal to drive while intoxicated, that is, to so put the lives of others at risk, surely it should be illegal to gestate while intoxicated, to similarly put the life of another at risk.

Such protection from harm and death would apply to third party actions as well. While not bound by promise, third parties are bound by the definition of the zygote/embryo/fetus as a preborn according to the woman's intent. Thus the hysterical husband-father who kicks a preborn through (and) a pregnant woman and who so kills it should, it seems to me, be held accountable for murder (as well as assault) – murder of a preborn, a new class of murder perhaps, but murder nevertheless. And the drunk driver who kills a woman and the preborn she was carrying should be accountable for *two* deaths.

Third party harm, especially when cumulative, would be harder to ascertain. For example, what about the second-hand cigarette smoke that causes harm? One person, one cigarette, does not cause significant harm; the amount that *does* cause significant harm will have come from various third parties. Do we hold the pregnant woman solely responsible? How reasonable is it to require that she leave the area? How reasonable is it to require that people refrain from smoking in the presence of a preborn? If 'the area' is her workplace, I believe the third parties' rights should be restricted – they should refrain from smoking. If 'the area' is the local pub, then the woman's rights should be restricted – she should not go to the pub.

The potentially born, on the other hand, would have no such rights. To say something is 'a potential X' is merely to state a possibility. It is not to predict; it is not to promise. Further, it is to state one possibility among many: a potential X is also a potential Y, or at the very least, a potential not-X. There are no grounds for claiming, then, that a potential X has *the right to become X* any more than it has the right to become Y or not-X. Thus a *potentially born* has no right to *be* born [12].

However, given that a potentially born *may become* a preborn, I think we have the same moral obligation not to harm it – at least until the decision has been made [13]. An exception should be made, however, for harm that causes pain to a potentially born that is sentient [14]: I think sentience alone provides sufficient grounds for the 'right' not to be subjected to unnecessary pain.

Lastly, considering abortion and prenatal harm together is *not* considering apples and not-apples together (a contradiction); it's considering apples and oranges: in the case of abortion, we're discussing quantity (of life – to have or not to have), but in the case of prenatal harm, we're discussing quality (of care – better or worse).

Having established the logical permissibility of legislating against prenatal harm without also having to legislate against abortion, I now turn to justifying such legislation. The strongest grounds for such legislation are consequential. One solid ground in favour of state rights at the prenatal stage, at least in Canada, is that the state has responsibility at the postnatal stage. Rights and responsibilities must go together: whoever has the *right to* do or not do X must be the same person who takes the *responsibility for* doing or not doing that X. Therefore, if one is unwilling to let the State say what a woman must or must not do for a child as a preborn (and recall that since the decision has been made to carry the fetus until it is a child, these terms can be used [15]), then one must also be unwilling to let the state do anything after for the child once it is born. Sole rights entail sole responsibilities. If the woman takes crack while pregnant (i.e. the state has no right to intervene), then the full cost for all medication, surgery, special schools, etc. needed for her brain-damaged child must be borne by her (i.e. the state has no responsibility to assist) [16]. This is a very contractual analysis and one that I think is fair – in theory.

In practice, however, my guess is that a woman who so 'abuses' her preborn child is not going to suddenly stop once it's born; she will *not*, therefore, pay for the necessary medication, surgery, etc. And so the child, clearly an innocent victim, will suffer – unless the state takes responsibility at that time. But it's quite unfair to expect the state ([and] the taxpayers) to stand idly by and watch the abuse and then expect it to clean up the mess.

Thus, when it cannot convincingly be shown that the mother will indeed take full responsibility for her actions toward the preborn, the State should be able to intervene, temporarily denying her full and usual rights, in the interests of justice *and* the child. If that requires institutionalizing the pregnant woman for nine months to ensure that she doesn't take crack and that the preborn does, in fact, become a healthy newborn, then so be it: that's the price she pays for her choice – she could've aborted [17].

---

1. Proudfoot, Madam Justice. "Judgement Respecting Female Infant 'D.J.'" in *Contemporary Moral Issues*, edited by Wesley Cragg. Toronto: McGraw-Hill Ryerson, 1992, pp.57-59.
2. Mathieu, Deborah. *Preventing Prenatal Harm: Should the State Intervene?* Dordrecht: Kluwer, 1991.
3. See also Kathleen Nolan ("Protecting Fetuses from Prenatal Hazards: Whose Crimes? What Punishment?" *Criminal Justice Ethics* 9/1 (1990):13-23) for a description of prenatal hazards and adverse effects of illicit drugs, tobacco, carbon monoxide, lead, alcohol, genetic conditions, infectious diseases, low birth weights, and treatment refusals.
4. Rachels, James. "Active and Passive Euthanasia" in *Ethics: Theory and Contemporary Issues*, edited by Barbara MacKinnon. Belmont: Wadsworth, 1995, pp.123-127. See also Thomas D. Sullivan, Philippa Foot, and others for discussion of the passive/active distinction.
5. Such countries include Czechoslovakia, France, Germany, Hungary, Italy, The Netherlands, Norway, Poland, Portugal, Rumania, U.S.S.R., and Turkey.
6. See Thomson for a discussion of 'minimally decent' and 'good' Samaritans.
7. See Bayles for discussion regarding the weighing of the prevention of harms against women's rights.
    See also Mathieu (52-54).
8. Streissguth, A.P., H.M.Barr, P.D.Sampson, et al. "IQ at Age 4 in Relation to Maternal Alcohol Use and Smoking During Pregnancy." *Developmental Psychology* 25, no.1 (1989): 7-9.
9. Callahan, Joan C. and James W. Knight, "On Treating Prenatal Harm as Child Abuse" in *Kindred Matters: Rethinking the Philosophy of the Family*, edited by Diana Tietjens Meyers, Kenneth Kipnis, and Cornelius F. Murphy, Jr. Ithaca: Cornell University Press, 1993, pp.143-170.
10. Feinberg, Joel. "A Question about Potentiality" in *Moral Issues*, edited by Jan Narveson. Toronto: Oxford, 1983, pp.234-238.
11. To say that a preborn has a *right* to life would mean also that I have a right to one of your kidneys (you promised). Or in the case of post-viability and Caesarean sections, it would mean also that I have a right to a kidney dialysis machine (the equivalent of the required life-sustaining incubator). On what grounds? Because I need

it? I'm not convinced that needs can establish rights. Because you promised? Promises can't establish rights either (we don't usually have a *right* to receive that which we're promised). But promises *can* establish moral obligations: one is simply morally obligated to keep one's promises. (The stronger promise of a contract might establish rights but contracts usually required two *consenting* parties.)

12. As for the 'future loss' injuries caused by abortion (the accusation made by Don Marquis), Narveson
(*Moral Matters*. Peterborough: Broadview Press, 1993) responds quite capably: "For if you abort fetus x, then there will *not* be, later on, some person who is worse off than she would have been had there been no abortion. If an abortion is performed now, there is later *no person at all* who grew from that fetus. And so there is no later person who is now harmed, by comparison with how she would have been had an abortion not taken place, no person whose right to life was violated very early on" (p. 184).

13. If the potentially born is to become an unborn/nonborn, then it seems odd indeed to even speak of harm – see previous note.

14. In an ideal world, a potentially born that is not to become a preborn would be aborted before sentience developed.

15. Normally, in abortion discussion, I object to 'preborn' 'child' as such terms load the argument.

16. The neonatal intensive care alone may cost $31,000; "estimates of the cost of life-long care for Fetal Alcohol Syndrome babies range from $600,000 to $2.5 million" (Oberman, Michelle. "Sex, Drugs, Pregnancy, and the Law: Rethinking the Problems of Pregnant Women who use Drugs" *Hastings Law Journal* 43 (1992):505-548).

17. She may well lose the child anyway – if she continues to use drugs which make her a negligent/abusive parent who causes harm to her child.

Telling our Members of Parliament What to Wear

So I recently found this on the Parliament of Canada website:
> While there is no Standing Order setting down a dress code for Members participating in debate, [84] Speakers have ruled that to be recognized to speak in debate, on points of order or during Question Period, tradition and practice require all Members, male or female, to dress in contemporary business attire. [85] The contemporary practice and unwritten rule require, therefore, that male Members wear a jacket, shirt and tie as standard dress. Clerical collars have been allowed, although ascots and turtlenecks have been ruled inappropriate for male Members participating in debate. [86] The Chair has even stated that wearing a kilt is permissible on certain occasions (for example, Robert Burns Day). [87] Members of the House who are in the armed forces have been permitted to wear their uniforms in the House. [88]

What could possibly justify this Speakers' rule?

Could it be that our Members of Parliament can't dress themselves? The people we've voted into positions of power? Doubtful. They're adults. Many of them even have a university degree. (Okay, I know ...)

Could it be somebody in a higher position of power is prioritizing appearance over reality? What you *look* like is more important than what you *are* like. That bodes well for – the world.

Could it be someone in a higher position of power is making a series of non sequiturs from clothing to behaviour and character? If you wear a business suit, you must be honest, hard-working, mature – respectable. Say what?

Could it be someone wants to maintain classist standards?

Generally speaking, the prescribed attire is more expensive than jeans and a t-shirt.

And the other thing to note? There's no mention of what exactly female members must wear [1]. Because there's no standard business attire for women? [2] No, that can't be right. Oh, oh, I know! Because there aren't supposed to *be* any women in Parliament!

---

1. " ... male Members wear a jacket, shirt and tie" (what, no trousers?)
2. The men must wear, essentially, a *business* suit. Because, or so, government is dominated by business (values, practices, etc.). [3]
3. Imagine if our members of parliament wore all sorts of attire (formal, casual) in all sorts of colour (yes, business is typically grey, black, brown, and navy). We'd get the sense of being represented by *real* (and diverse) people (not just profit puppets) ...

The Problem with Democracy

The problem with democracy is that it's just an appeal to the majority.

And most people, the majority, simply want whatever's in their *own* best interest. We are a nation of egoists. Average life span what it is, personal interests are necessarily short-term. Average intelligence what it is, personal interests are also immediate and concrete. So what's good for the whole, the whole country, never mind the whole planet, will never happen.

So talk about the need for an informed citizenry is irrelevant. True, at any given time, the majority doesn't know diddlysquat. But also true, they have no interest whatsoever in finding out. Because all they care about is themselves. And they're convinced they already know all there is to know about what's best for themselves. And they're probably right, because their interests are so directly and immediately served.

Worse, many of the few to whom one might speak about the problem with this state of affairs believe that the good of the whole is equal to the good of the parts; so, they reason, this state of affairs, each individual voting for what he or she personally wants, is the best state of affairs.

I suppose it might be the most fair, the most just, state of affairs – which only means that when our world stops working, we will have gotten exactly what we deserve.

We, the majority, that is.

Snowmobiles Rule – Only in Canada. Pity.

Snowmobilers are often presented as people who enjoy the natural beauty of the North. Oh please. Not while their exhaust pipes spew fumes into our air. And their tossed beer cans litter the trail until someone else picks them up. Not at the speeds they drive. And their engines roar at a volume that must be endured by everyone within five miles.

What snowmobiling *is* all about adolescent males going VROOM VROOM.

Which means that our government has handed over thousands of miles [1] of crown land – designated snowmobile trails – to a bunch of young men to use as their personal racetrack. How fair is that? And did they ask us first?

When a friend of mine contacted the MNR to ask about putting up signs at each end of a path through crown land that snowmobilers are using as a short cut to get to their trail and, in the process, making it dangerous (not to mention extremely unpleasant because of the fumes and the noise) for the rest of us to use (for walking and cross-country skiing), she was told no, they can't put up signs prohibiting snowmobilers from using it because everyone has access to crown land. Right. Then why do the signs on the snowmobile trails say 'No Trespassing – You must have a permit to use this trail'?

Why has the government done this? Because they're adolescent males themselves. Who still want to go VROOM VROOM.

And because local businesses asked them to, because they want to make money from the snowmobilers.

Snowmobilers are a minority. Local business owners are a minority. Why do they get to determine policy and practice? Policy and practice that affects other people?

When snowmobilers (and ATVers and dirtbikers – essentially, all motorized recreational vehicles) use crown land the way they want, no one else can use it the way they want. Consider the trails, mentioned above, that are now unsafe and unpleasant for hikers and skiers. Consider the lake we all live on; in winter (and in summer too – jetskis, another motorized recreational vehicle), our properties may as well be backing on, well, a racetrack. (So much for sitting outside and – well, so much for sitting outside. Not to mention canoeing or kayaking.) Consider all the backroads we live on, the ones without sidewalks. It's nice that we can hear a snowmobile coming from miles away so we have time to get off the road, but it's not enough to get off to the side (assuming that's not where we already are), because that's where the snowmobiles drive. It's not even enough to get *off* the road and up onto the snowbank, because they like to ride the banks. You have to climb up and *over* the snowbanks to be safe. In some countries, pedestrians have the right of way. In Canada, fume-spewing (and gas-guzzling), noise-farting, male-driven snowmobiles do.

---

1. Ontario alone has 18,641 miles (30,000 km) of designated snowmobile trails, though some of that goes through (with permission) private and municipal land.

Rich Rednecks

I think it's about time we toss out the idea that those in manual labour are lower class – not quite as 'well off' as those in, say, management and the so-called 'professions'.

He's got a new pickup. They're not cheap. About $40,000. My used Saturn cost $9,000.

His truck gets about 15 mpg. My Saturn gets about 40 mpg. And gas isn't cheap. (And yet he seems to get in that truck of his at the drop of a hat. I ration my trips into town.)

He's got an ATV. And a snowmobile. And a jetski. Let's say $10,000 each, give or take, that makes $30,000. I've got a used laptop and high-speed internet. $1,000.

He smokes. And drinks. (I've never actually seen him do either, but I've been picking up his beer cans and cigarette butts on the trails for years now.) That's gotta add up.

Oh but he can't afford to send his kid to university. And he's in debt, eh, 'cuz he hasn't got one of them high-paying jobs, right, so give him a break!

How to Make a Man Grow Up

I was recently surprised to discover that in the U.S., men are required by law to register for the "selective service system".

Only men. I thought women were allowed in their military now.

And *required*. I didn't think they had 'the draft' anymore.

When I expressed my surprise, hoping to engage someone in conversation, the guy in line behind me (I was in a U.S. post office, where the brochures reminding men of their duty were prominently displayed) said that he agreed that it should be mandatory to serve for two years: "It makes 'em 'grow up'."

Hm. How does teaching someone to kill make a person grow up? That is, what's mature about learning how to kill? What's mature about actually killing?

Of course, being in the military isn't just about killing. Arguably. But what's mature about being pressured to conform, to obey orders?

Sure, the forced routine, of physical exercise and psychological effort, might become a habit. And that's a good thing. A grown-up thing. But there are other, far better, ways to achieve that same result.

And sure, the presumed altruism – you're serving your country, life's not all about you – is good, mature. But again, is killing someone really the best example of altruism we can put before young men? Young men who need to grow up?

It seems to me the selective service system is a bad way to fix a bunch of other bad ways.

The question we have to ask is how do boys *get* to eighteen *without* growing up?

Rules of Combat

Why are there rules of combat? Rules apply to civil interactions and games. Combat is neither.

Rules give the impression of fairness, decency, civility. They thus make war permissible.

But if war is really about defending your loved ones, wouldn't you do whatever is necessary? Wouldn't you 'fight dirty' if that's what it takes?

Rules of combat suggest, therefore, that war isn't about defending your loved ones. Or even your land, your water, your resources. As Allan G. Johnson points out, in the best analysis of men and war I've ever read (*The Gender Knot,* p.138-142), "war allows men to reaffirm their masculine standing in relation to other men … . It is an opportunity for men to bond with other men – friend and foe alike – and reaffirm their common masculine warrior codes. If war was simply about self-sacrifice in the face of monstrous enemies who threaten men's loved ones, how do we make sense of the long tradition of respect between wartime enemies, the codes of 'honor' that bind them together even as they bomb and devastate civilian populations that consist primarily of women and children?" Good question. So (and this explains the response to women in the military [1]), war is really all about men getting together and hating, hurting, killing women.

Same old same old.

---

1. Exclusion. Rape.

Responding to Wolf-Whistles

Many men will wolf-whistle at *any* woman. [1]

So it's not so much an insult to a particular woman [2] as an indication of the man's insecurity about his manhood: he feels the need to assure himself and/or others [3], *since his behaviour is public*, that he's a *man*. Apparently, to such men, finding women sexually attractive is proof of manhood. *Heterosexual* manhood. So really the wolf-whistle is an indication of homophobia.

So rather than focus on the inherent misogyny, we should focus on his insecurity. And, therefore, we should respond with something like "Don't use me to deal with your insecurity about 'being a man'!"

Granted, most men won't understand that, so you'll have to simplify and expand with something like "I understand that you're afraid that your friends think you're gay, but don't use me to deal with that fear. Just talk to your friends; tell them you're not gay."

(Right. Like that's ever gonna happen.)

And those who *are* smart enough to understand our initial response will be so resistant they won't process it. Because introspection, self-awareness – these are not part of the definition of manhood. [4]

(Sigh.)

---

1. And once women realize that, perhaps they'll give up the make-up, the dress, the body obsession: *to men, it really doesn't matter how you look.*
2. Yes, men, wolf-whistles are insulting when they occur in everyday contexts – because they emphasize our sexuality when we're trying to be seen for our personhood and our various competencies; it thus *reduces* us to sexual objects. A wolf-whistle in the bedroom directed toward your consenting sexual partner is, can be, a completely

different matter.
3. Other *men*.
4. My father *hated* it whenever I tried to get him to examine his behaviour. "Are you trying to psychoanalyze me?" he'd shout. As if I was proposing castration. (I suspect that like most men, he was afraid I'd discover there's nothing much there; men spend so much time thinking about strategy, they haven't developed any genuine core.)

Just tell me what to say and I'll say it

"What do you want me to say?" your pre-Nigel, Nigel, or ex-Nigel says helplessly, having obviously said the wrong thing, again. "Just tell me what to say and I'll say it."

I want you to say what you think. And if I don't agree with it, then I'm outta here. It's that simple. (Because why would I want a relationship, a friendship, with someone with whom I don't agree? On the important things. Maybe even on the unimportant things.)

Why is it so hard for so many men to just say what they really think? Because they don't know. They are so supremely unaccustomed to introspection.

Because, in any case, the truth is irrelevant, useless. That's why it's so difficult for them to know what to say. "What do you want me to say?" means "What lies will work here?"

They think that their relationship with you is all, and only, about sexual access, recreational and reproductive. And they're willing to say whatever it takes to get that access. To seduce is to manipulate. [1]

And guys, if that's how you get a date, a girlfriend, a wife – by figuring out 'the right thing' to say – are you really surprised that it doesn't last? That one day she realizes you're bullshit through and through, have been since the beginning?

---

1. Why doesn't it occur to men that if the woman really wanted them, they wouldn't have to seduce her, they wouldn't have to manipulate her?

The Last Man on Earth Explains Everything

The Last Man on Earth explains everything. But he's too stupid, too infantile, and too self-centered, to know it. Which is exactly why he explains everything.

1. *He enjoys knocking things over, breaking things, destroying things.*

He rams his grocery cart into a pyramid of cans. He rolls bowling balls into a row of aquariums. [1] Apparently delighted to hear the smash. His reaction to blowing up one car with another is orgasmic. What does that tell us? *Destroying things gives men pleasure.*

2. *He wantonly pollutes the water. That is to say, he does not use resources responsibly. And that is to say, he exhibits extremely short-sighted thinking.*

He uses a swimming pool for a toilet. [2] A metaphor if there ever was one. In more ways than one. (In addition to the despoiling of resources, it shows us how full of shit he is.) (And that he is, quite literally, an asshole.)

He does this, perhaps, because he figures he can just move into a new house whenever he's finished wrecking the one he's in. [3] Again, such a metaphor. (We've used up our own water and oil, so let's go to someone else's country and use up theirs.) (And when we've used up Earth, we'll go live on the Moon.)

Is it that, like other infants, Phil doesn't understand "All gone!"? [4]

Is it that he lacks the ability to imagine the long-term consequences of his behaviour?

And does he really think he's the only one left? What a special little snowflake he is. Sure, he drove all over the country. Calling out from an RV. Real thorough. Apparently, he didn't consider the possibility that someone might be alive, but be hurt or in other need of help that would require him to actually *get out of the RV* and *walk around* a bit.

But that's Phil. He thinks the world is all about him now. (Actually, he's probably thought that all along.)

3. *He doesn't really do much else.*

Well, he eats a lot of junk food. And he drinks a lot of alcohol.

4. *He thinks about himself.*

He thinks about how lonely he is. Which may seem paradoxical, given how incapable he is of thinking about other people. But he's incapable of thinking about what other people might *need* or *want*. He's lonely because of what *he* needs and wants. (Which explains why, when he finds himself so utterly alone, his cry sounds more like the wail of an infant than an existential scream. [5])

No surprise, then, that

5. *He considers half the human species merely as things to be fucked.*

Almost the first words we hear him say are about how much he misses women. Since that comes right after apologies to God for masturbating so much, we know he misses women because he uses them to masturbate. (Not because they might know the cure for the virus.)

And just in case we missed this, we see him choosing porn over food in the grocery store [6], and we see his lingering gaze at the female-bodied mannequin.

So that's three times in the first six minutes we get this message: women are sexual objects for his use. [7]

When he dreams about a woman eagerly kissing him, the woman is, of course, gorgeous. Why is it that unattractive men always think women will find them attractive? More incredibly, why is it that *un*attractive men think *attractive* women will find them attractive? Seriously. How deluded do you have to be about your own attractiveness? [8]

And again, just in case we missed this, when Carol introduces herself as "the last woman on Earth," we see from the look on his face that he's thinking he may have to break the bro pledge, "I wouldn't fuck her if she was the last woman on earth."

Phil thinks he's the last man on Earth because some virus wiped out everyone else. That may have been the proximate cause. (Or just bad writing.) It's likely that climate change, due to melting polar ice, due to increased greenhouse gases, due to relentless fossil fuel use and meat consumption, changed disease vectors which, along with the consequent disruption in the supply of goods and services (food, water, drugs; medical care) created a perfect storm for the virus to become a global epidemic.

He's the last man on Earth because he gets pleasure from destroying things, because he doesn't live responsibly, because he thinks only of himself, his own (primarily physical) needs and wants HERE! and NOW! – in short, because he's disgustingly infantile.

I don't find that at all entertaining, let alone insightful, so I stopped watching. [9, 10]

---

1. And of course, he won't clean up the broken glass. But, well, he's the last man on Earth, and, hey, if he doesn't bother him ... So if, when, he discovers he's *not* the last person on Earth, if, when, he discovers there are other people in the world, other people who might want to walk there without getting cut up, will he go back *then* and clean up the mess he made? Of course he will. And pigs will fly.
2. It brings to mind the patch of garbage floating around in the Pacific Ocean that's twice the size of the United States. And all the industrial waste – 70% of it – that men (most likely) pour directly into our fresh water.
3. The truly disgusting shape of the house he's living in after a mere five months brings to mind that thing about if the history of the Earth were a year, life wouldn't appear until March, multi-cellular organisms not until November, we'd show up on December 31, by late evening, we'd have well-developed brains – and then it'd take us a mere forty seconds to thoroughly trash the place.
4. He glories in there being no rules or, more specifically, in there being no rule-enforcer: like a child, he hasn't developed any rules of his own.

5. That he continues to believe there's a God also indicates just how child-like Phil is. He may as well be writing Dear Santa letters.
6. That pornographic magazines, magazines in which women are for the most part humiliated and degraded, are openly for sale, even in grocery stores, without disapproval by the writers or Phil is clear evidence of the rampant misogyny I'm pointing out.
7. It's pretty much what the writers think about women. In the very first episode, we see there's also a woman alive. But is the series titled, then, *The Last Man* and Woman *on Earth?* Of course not. Women are not worth mention. (Well, except, as fuckholes.)
8. But of course, whether or not the woman is attracted to doesn't even cross his mind; can we say 'rapist mentality'?
9. Who *does* find that entertaining? And *why*?
10. And does *anyone* find it insightful? I mean, really, is *any* of this *news*?

13 Reasons Why: How to Make a Movie without acknowledging the Elephant in the Room

So I've just finished watching *13 Reasons Why* and am struck by the completely unacknowledged elephant in the room. *Not one character* acknowledges that almost all of the problems leading to Hannah's suicide stem from sexism and its many tumours – misogyny, male entitlement, male privilege, hypersexualization, objectification, the rape culture, etc., etc., etc.

Consider:

Justin – Being a man is all about getting sex, using women for sex, and bragging about it afterwards to get points, to improve your status (among males). Exaggerating and lying about your 'achievements' is, well, standard operating procedure if you're a guy. 'Bros before hos' – even if it means letting your girlfriend be raped (because hey, what's mine is yours) (and women are just property, after all) (otherwise, it wouldn't even have occurred to him that what he 'owed' Bryce could include Jessica). That said, (weak) applause for his eventual decency, especially given his relative-to-Bryce lack of privilege and the pull of moral obligation for reciprocity (albeit disgustingly overgeneralized, as mentioned).

Jessica – Men are more important than women. One, getting a boyfriend is the most important thing you can do, being someone's girlfriend is the most important thing you can be; your status, your value, depends on your relation to a male – which is why as soon as she and Alex hook up, Hannah is dropped like a second-class piece of shit. Two, what men say is to be believed, they are authorities, about everything; when they open their mouths, truth tumbles out like little golden nuggets – which is why she believes what she's told by Alex et al about Hannah. Three, she's a cheerleader. Her actual 'job' is to cheer and applaud men when they do stuff. (In fact, many of the girls in *13 Reasons Why* are cheerleaders, and many of the boys are jocks. A whole 90% of the student body is missing. Why? Give you one guess.) (Actually, on second thought, strictly speaking, that's not true. Of the eight boys listed here, only three are jocks. So why did I get that wrong impression? Because they appear as a group, wearing uniforms. They appear as a team, a gang, a team, an army. That's why they seem more … powerful.)

Alex – Women are to be evaluated solely on the basis of their body parts, on whether their body parts please you/men. Again, (weak) applause for his regret and guilt, and his speaking up, but, yeah, men like Alex who confront men like Bryce will get beaten up. Thus, his limited confrontation and his suicide attempt can also be traced to the fucked-up patriarchal culture.

Tyler – Women's bodies are public domain; ergo, photographs of women's bodies are public domain. It's not like there's a person inside or anything.

Courtney – Being lesbian in public means you risk 'corrective rape'; can we blame her for hiding?

Marcus – When a girl agrees to meet you for a milkshake, she's really agreeing to have sex with you. At the very least, she's agreeing to have her genitals fondled by you. In public. In broad daylight. And certainly in the presence of the bros you brought along to witness your conquest. If she objects, well, your outrage is justified. Because you're *entitled* to touch her. In fact, you're entitled to touch any woman. Any time, any place. Simply because you're a man.

Zach – She doesn't particularly like you? She rejected your advances of friendship? Well, yeah, FUCK HER! Because

men are entitled to the affection of all women.
Ryan – Sure it's okay to publish someone's work without their permission, without crediting them, perhaps especially if they're a woman and you're a man. Because you, men, know best. What's best for her, women. (Oh, and thanks for carrying on the great tradition of 'Anon' …)
Sheri – Perhaps the *only* episode that *doesn't* implicate the elephant.
Bryce – Women don't know what they want, but you, *you, a MAN* (well, a boy), *you* know what they want. (And they *all* want you. They all want your penis inside them.) (At least, you "*assume* so.") (And that's good enough.) Thanks to the patriarchy, you can be appallingly deluded about your knowledge and your appeal. You can lie to yourself about it. Again and again.
Mr. Porter – Yes, he goes to regretted sex first, then to alcohol and drugs, but when he gets to rape, Hannah says she didn't tell Bryce to stop, she says she didn't tell him 'No' – so what's he supposed to think? He suggests she may have consented then changed her mind (which she's certainly entitled to do) (and which still leaves the door open to rape), then asks whether they should get her parents or the police involved, but she says 'No' – again, what's he supposed to think or do? And *of course*, he can't promise that Bryce will go to jail. Guess why. He tells her it may be 'best to move on' (but only after he clarifies that Hannah won't give a name, she won't press charges, she's not even sure she *can* press charges), showing that he too is caught in the mire of our fucked-up patriarchy.
Clay – Clay buys into the Prince Charming shit: he blames himself for not saving Hannah. (He doesn't blame himself for not saving Alex – though perhaps he doesn't know yet …) Near the end, he says something like 'We need to start

treating each other better, we need to start caring about each other.' Well, as Bryce would surely tell him, caring about others is for sissies – females. And in a patriarchy, male values trump female values (and yes, in a patriarchy there's a difference).

Hannah – She exhibits a lot of passivity, a persistent denial of agency. She wants Clay to kiss her; why doesn't she want to kiss him? (She wants to be kissed; she doesn't want to kiss.) She wants Clay to ask her to dance; why doesn't she just ask him to dance? She wants him to be her Valentine; why doesn't she just tell him that? She tells Clay to go away, but then expects him to stay. Not only is he not a mind reader, but it's that kind of shit that got us to 'no means yes'. (Tony had it right: she asked him to go, he should go, end of story.) Standing outside Mr. Porter's office, she waits to be saved, for him to come running after her.

And of course as soon as Bryce, whom she'd *seen* rape Jessica, gets into the hot tub, she doesn't get out. She probably didn't want to appear rude. You know, hurt his feelings. Once he begins, she doesn't scream STOP; she doesn't scream NO. She just ... accepts it, endures it. (And 'it' looks like it might have been sodomy, not 'just' PIV rape.) That's what women, girls, are supposed to do. That's what we're raised to do.

If the girls wore alarm necklaces (instead of short little genitals-easily-accessible skirts) she could've pulled its pin (like a grenade) when she saw Bryce start to rape Jessica ... And again when she was in the hot tub ... And, backing up a bit, why do we keep our teenaged girls so clueless, so desperate (for ... what?) that *they get into a hot tub at a party at a rapist's house in just their bra and panties* (let alone *go to a party at his place in the first place*)? Not to mention, of course, why do we keep our teenaged boys so clueless the moral wrongness of patriarchy, sexism, misogyny, male entitlement, male privilege ...

So the thirteen reasons why pretty much boil down to one. And it's not even acknowledged.

Feminists have exposed and fought against patriarchy, sexism, misogyny, male entitlement, male privilege, hypersexualization, objectification, rape culture – hell, we *named* most of that shit – for decades. Not acknowledged. Not once. Not even a little bit. It's like Jay Asher was born yesterday and has remained oblivious of such women's voices. Ironic. To say the least.

(I cheered when 'the male gaze' was actually mentioned by the girls – but then they got it wrong, they made it sound like it just describes the attracted look on a guy's face.) (Oh for the love of God!)

And another thing. There are no doubt hundreds of *13 Reasons Why* novels written by women. Have any of them been published? Made into a movie? Received great critical claim? No. But a *man* writes about what it's like to be raped, what it's like to be subjected to misogynistic shit every fucking day, well, world, PAY ATTENTION! Asher is himself a shining example of the male privilege his novel criticizes so unwittingly. Again, the irony.

Furthermore, how many more Sylvia Plaths do we need to see? Why must we keep seeing women kill themselves because of this shit? Why can't we see as many, if not more, saying FUCK THIS SHIT!? Yes, okay, Jessica was drunk, and Hannah isn't a cheerleader, but why couldn't Asher have reversed that? Because, hey, if a girl can do four back handsprings (without mats even), she surely has the strength (shoulders, abs, legs) and the courage (without mats, remember?) to fight back at least *a little*. Why didn't we see a sober cheerleader, or two or three, bustin' Bryce's ass when he tried his shit. Why don't we see more movies like Jodi Foster's *The Brave One*? Give you one guess.

Never mind the elephant. *13 Reasons Why* is a trojan horse.

SlutWalk: What's the problem?

What exactly is the problem with SlutWalk? The event was reportedly initiated in response to a police officer's comment about not dressing like a slut if you don't want to get raped. The underlying assumption is that one's attire – specific items or style – sends a message. And indeed it does. High heels, fishnet stockings, and a heavily made-up face are considered invitations. So if a woman is wearing 'fuck me shoes', she can hardly complain if someone fucks her.

But *is* that the message the woman is sending? A message that she's sexually available to everyone? Maybe. Maybe not. [1] Frankly, given the ambiguity, and the nature of the outcome in the case of misunderstanding, I wonder why women take the risk.

It's much like wearing one's gang colours in the territory of a rival gang. Of course it's going to be provocative. Is any consequent assault legal? No. Is it deserved? No. Should it have been anticipated? Yes. So unless the intent was to make a point about the wrongness of gangs and violence, a point best made by arranging media presence *for* the incursion into the other gang's territory, well, *how stupid are you*?

Granted, most women who dress in a sexually attractive way don't go that far (fishnet stockings and heavy make-up), but why go any way at all? Why *does* a woman dress in a sexually attractive way? Why do women put on high heels, show their legs, wear bras that push up their breasts and tops that expose cleavage, redden their lips, and so on? What does she hope to *attract* exactly?

My first guess is that she hasn't thought about it. She dresses in a sexually attractive way because, well, that's what women in our society are expected to do. [2] In which case she's an idiot.

Doesn't deserve to be raped, but really, she should think about what she does.

My second guess is that she dresses in a sexually attractive way because she wants to attract *offers of* sex. [3] But then, she shouldn't be angry when she *receives* such offers, either in the form of whistles and call-outs or in more direct ways. That she may respond with anger or offense suggests that she wants to attract only offers she's likely to accept, offers only from men she's attracted to. But, men may cry, how's a man to know? Um, try to make eye contact. If you can't do that, she's not interested. If you *do* make eye contact, smile. If she doesn't smile back, she's not interested. Surely that kind of body language isn't too subtle to grasp.

And yet, many men seem to have such an incapacity for subtlety that if you act like bait, they may simply reach out and grab you. Are they entitled to do that? No. Any unauthorized touching is a violation. Is clothing authorization? Well, sometimes. Consider uniforms.

So it would be far less ambiguous if a woman who wants sex just extended the offers herself. Why take the passive route of inviting offers from likely candidates? Why make men try to figure out whether they're a likely candidate? Why not just let them know and go from there?

Another problem with SlutWalk is that many people may not have been aware of the police officer's comment. So what are they to make of the event? What are they to understand is the point? (Prerequisite to deciding whether to support it or not.)

    (a) "It's okay to be a slut!" Given the 'sluttish' appearance that many women present during the walk, this understanding is understandable. But whether or not one wants to endorse that message depends on the definition of 'slut.' [4]

    (b) "We're proud to be sluts!" Ditto.

(c) "No woman deserves to be raped, regardless of her attire!" This is probably closest to the intended message, but in this case, better to have called it a "Walk Against Rape". Better, further, to advocate changes that would make rape more likely to be reported and rapists more likely to be sentenced commensurate to the injuries they've caused. Perhaps better still to advocate a male-only curfew.

Of course, "SlutWalk" is far more provocative, far more attention-getting, than the ho-hum "Walk Against Rape", but I don't think the organizers considered the difficulty of reclaiming an insulting word. And 'slut' is a very difficult insult to reclaim. Harder than 'bitch' and 'nigger' (sex trumps skin color; better to be a black man than a white woman) and even those reclamation efforts haven't been very successful. Mostly, success has been limited to conversations among women in the first case and conversations among blacks in the second. SlutWalk is not conducted in the presence of women only. So, really, did the organizers expect people in general to accept (let alone understand) their implied redefinition?

The organizers also didn't think through the male over-dependence on visual signals. The gawkers and hecklers who typically undermine the event should be expected. The inability of men to process any verbal messages (even those just a few words long) in the presence of so-called 'fuck me' heels should be expected.

Consider that even Gwen Jacobs' action to make it legal for women to be shirtless wasn't immune to sexualization, despite the clearly non-sexual nature of her action; men (BOOBS!) hooted, men (BOOBS!) called out, and the media, no doubt reflecting a decision made by a man (BOOBS!), or perhaps a thoughtless woman, *continues* to use the sexualized "topless" instead of "shirtless" when reporting about the issue (BOOBS!). Imagine the response had Jacobs gone shirtless while also wearing short shorts exposing half buttocks. It would have been, to understate, a mixed message.

And that is, essentially, the problem with SlutWalk. High heels, exposed legs, pushed-up breasts, and a made-up faces sends a message that one is sexually available (which is why it's appalling to me that it has become convention for women to wear heels and make-up in public every day all day) (those who *accept* that convention accept the view that women *should* be, or at least should *seem* to be, sexually available every day all day). [5] And if it doesn't send a message that you're sexually available, what message *does* it send? That you're sexually *attractive*? Back to the top – *what are you hoping to attract?* (And why are you trying to attract that when you're at work, working?)

(d) "Women have a right to tease!" *That* seems to be the message SlutWalk conveys, given the likelihood that women who present themselves as sexually attractive *aren't* actually trying to be sexually attractive to everyone or, at least, aren't sexually *available* to everyone. And that's a message that many women would *not* endorse. Especially those who know about the provocation defence [6].

There's nothing wrong with extending invitations to sex. Doing so in public in such a non-specific way – that's the problem. Especially given men's inability to pick up on subtle cues and/or their refusal to understand the difference between yes and no, let alone yes and maybe. Maybe when men can handle a sexually charged atmosphere without assaulting ... Maybe when other men penalize, one way or another, those who can't handle a sexually charged atmosphere without assaulting ...

In the meantime, we're living in an occupied country, a country occupied by morally-underdeveloped people with power who think women are just walking receptacles for their dicks. So women who make themselves generally available, or present themselves as being generally available, are, simply, putting themselves at great risk (and, yes, in a way, getting what they asked for): some STDs are fatal; others are incurable; most have painful symptoms. And pregnancy has a life-long price tag. [7]

---

1. Given that the values and norms are different for men than for women and given that we are neither accustomed nor socialized to giving (or requesting) explicit consent for sex, it's essential to be clear about the signals of 'implied consent'. It's also almost impossible: the signals, ranging from mere presence to attire to a gesture to a look, are ambiguous and variably sent/received – some men assume mere presence in their apartment means 'yes', some do not; some women intend a certain outfit to mean 'yes', some do not. Even on the few occasions when consent may be given or withheld explicitly, men may understand 'no' to mean 'yes'. And indeed, given the socialization discussed earlier, a woman *may* mean 'yes' when she says 'no'. As Margaret Jane Radin puts it (in "The Pragmatist and the Feminist"), 'Just say no' as the standard for determining whether rape has occurred is both under- and over-inclusive. It is under-inclusive because women who haven't found their voices mean 'no' and are unable to say it; and it is over-inclusive because, like it or not, the way sexuality has been constituted in a culture of male dominance, the male understanding that 'no' means 'yes' was often, and may still sometimes be, correct.

However, as Susan Estrich points out (in "Rape"), "the 'no means yes' philosophy ... affords sexual enjoyment to those women who desire it but will not say so – at the cost of violating the integrity of all those women who say 'no' and mean it" [2]. This is the minefield when 'group membership' is 'mandatory' (when females are considered a group – women): if there is no room for individual subjectivity, serious errors will be made.

2. There's a difference between attractive and *sexually* attractive. At least, there *should* be. Perhaps because men dominate art and advertising, the two have been equivocated. (No doubt because *everything* is sexual for them.) (Which may be to say, everything is about dominance for them.)

3. Maybe part of her smiles to think of herself as a slut. She's a bad girl, she's dangerous, she's taking risks, she's a wild girl for once in her life. But that's exactly what they want. Sexual access. No-strings-attached sex. We fell for that in the 60s too. Free love, sure, we're not prudes, we're okay with our bodies, we're okay with sex, we're 'with it'. But they never took us seriously. They never considered us part of the movement. Behind our backs, they'd snicker and say the best position for a woman is prone (Stokely Carmichael). (Read your history, learn about our past.)

4. See "What's wrong with being a slut?" (Also in *Sexist Shit that Pisses Me Off.*)

5. Of course there's the possibility that if/when women forego the heels, bared legs, accentuated breasts and butts, and make-up, men will consider a little ankle to be an open invitation. Which just means the issue isn't attire *at all*. It's being *female*. In a patriarchy. (Which still means SlutWalk is off-target.)

6. Also in *Sexist Shit that Pisses Me Off.*

7. I hear the objections already: 'No, wearing high heels and make-up *doesn't* mean I'm sexually available! *That's* the point!' (And around and around we go.) Then why do you wear high heels and make-up? Seriously, think about it: high heels make the leg more shapely, attracting the male gaze, which follows your legs up … ; make-up makes your face younger, hence more sexually attractive; lipstick attracts the male gaze to your lips, your mouth … If you just want to be attractive, then what you do to your body wouldn't be sexualized: you'd wear funky gold glittered hiking boots, you'd paint an iridescent rainbow across your face, you'd do a hundred *other* aesthetically interesting things …

Stop Being Complicit in your own Subordination

Although the cautionary 'Don't blame the victim' is important in the context of assault, especially sexual assault, especially in a sexist society in which women are typically blamed more than men (and why is that, exactly?), I think we have overgeneralized.

And although I would certainly put more blame on men than on women for our sexist society, because it is men who are in a position of dominance (with greater power comes greater responsibility), I do think women are often to blame. We have agency. We are not idiots. And often we are *not* coerced.

And yet, often, we are complicit in our own subordination. We speak in a higher register than is actually necessary and thus come across as child-like. We smile more often than we need to and thus cancel the importance of our words. We endorse the importance of our appearance by wearing make-up to cover blemishes and wrinkles and by constantly dieting. Worse, we emphasize the sexuality of our appearance – by reddening our lips, emphasizing our breasts [1], exposing our legs – as a matter of *daily routine*. [2]

No one coerces us to do any of that. Coercion is implicated when you allow yourself to be assaulted by your live-in partner because that's the only way to feed your kids, when you do not refuse because someone has drugged you, and when you shut the fuck up because otherwise he'll kill you. Coercion is *not* implicated when you wear make-up, high heels, and an easy-access dress.

Cultural conditioning, social expectation, peer pressure – why go along with it all? Why not think for yourself? Consider the meanings, the implications, of what you do. For yourself. For others. And have the courage to refuse, to reject, whatever makes you into something you don't want to be.

I'm suspect of claims that one would be fired if one stopped performing femininity. (Try doing so in small increments.) (Try suing.) I imagine that yes, one might not be *hired* for some jobs if one doesn't perform femininity, but if possible, apply for a job somewhere else. And yes, since Hooters pays more than Walmart, I may be asking you to make a sacrifice – for the greater good.

Because only when men *don't* see us as hooters will the female sales associate at Walmart be considered for a managerial position. It seems to be all or nothing: if men see us as sexual, they see us as *only* sexual; if we have sexual power, we won't have any other kind of power – political, economic, social. It's understandable to think otherwise, but most women realize, once they hit forty and whatever sexual attractiveness they had wanes, that any power they had to that point *was* in fact merely due to their sex, their sexuality. Not their knowledge, their ability, their competence.

So please, don't use your sex, or your sexuality, to get what you want. It makes it harder for the rest of us to be considered *persons,* with interests and abilities other than having sex and having kids. [3]

Yes, I know you *can* use your sexuality to get what you want. Men are idiot children when it comes to breasts, butts, and legs.

But make no mistake. They are in power. Over us. They own most of the property, they hold most of the managerial positions, they hold most of the political positions, they make more money than we do … And they typically don't concern themselves with ethics [4] and that adds to their power: they will not hesitate to hurt us. Just take a look at contemporary porn, which is, thanks to the internet, viewed by most men, many of whom started when they were still kids. (You are, you become, what you expose yourself to.)

So please, just *don't* do it. Don't speak in your little girl voice. Don't smile at everything and everyone. Don't wear make-up and heels. Don't even expose your legs. Unless you're sure you're not being sexual about it (which means don't shave). Present yourself as a person, not specifically a *female* person.

And don't expect a man to pay your way for anything. Only invalids and children need to have someone else pay their way. Don't even accept it because you think he's just being nice. He's not paying your way to be nice. He's paying your way to express his superiority (just watch how angry he gets when *you* insist on paying *his* way) and to underscore your need for him, your dependence on him.

Don't get married for the badge of maturity. It makes it that much harder for those of us who see marriage as the sexist trap it is: the unmarried are treated like children, perpetual teenagers who haven't yet grown up.

And unless you really like kids (did you want to become a nursery school teacher?), don't have them. It too is a badge of maturity and your endorsement of that irrationality makes it that much harder for those of us who choose to be child-free to be seen as adults. It too is a trap. In fact, in our society, there is no stronger, no more complete, trap into subordination. Because then you *will* need him. Then you *will* become dependent on him. Which will triple his power over you. [5] And kids make you vulnerable. Oh so vulnerable to threat, to blackmail, in all its subtle forms.

So just don't. Don't be complicit in your own subordination.

---

1. A 'plunging' neckline points like an arrow to breasts that are likely padded and pushed up – is it any wonder you find yourself saying "My eyes are up here"? Talk about a mixed message.
2. What if it were convention for men to wear their shirts with the sleeves rolled up and the top few buttons undone and to wear make-up that accentuated their jaw and cheek

lines? Would they get chest hair implants and start obsessing about the muscularity of their forearms? Would they consider facial reconstruction surgery? And would women ever take them seriously?

3. I'll respond in advance to everyone who's thinking that I'm a prude, that I'm anti-sex, that I don't like sex. You know what? You're right. I *am* anti-sex. I *don't* like sex. *Not as it typically occurs today.* Which is primarily *for men's pleasure*, often via women's pain (physical and psychological – anal penetration, vaginal penetration without sufficient lubrication, often accompanied by humiliation, degradation, insult …). Sex *for women's pleasure* wouldn't even *involve* the penis! The clitoris (which is not in the vagina or the rectum) best responds to fingers.

While I'm at it, I'll also respond in advance to those women who reprimand me for abandoning the sisterhood. Excuse me? You are not my sister. We are accidentally the same sex. You have embraced the gender that society aligns with your sex. I have not. You're a woman. I am not. (And that you wonder, mocking, laughing, 'Well what *are* you?' indicates the depth of your internalization of the importance of sex. To everything. Including, most especially, your *identity*.)

4. Even *speaking up* about doing the right thing gets them accused of being a wuss, of going soft. Which apparently is more than most men can bear.

5. Because look, you can't take your infant to work with you, so you *will* need someone to look after it while you're out earning rent, and that will cost, probably as much, or almost as much, as you make, so you *still* won't have rent … Better to form an alliance with another mother; you can work eight hours at your job while she looks after yours and hers, then she can work eight hours at her job while you look after hers and yours.

This is your brain. This is your brain on oxytocin: Mom.

I think many women realize that their children make them vulnerable; their love for them holds them hostage. So many things they would do (leave?) – but for the children. I wonder how many realize that their imprisonment is partly (largely?) physiological. And, in most cases, as voluntary as that first hit of heroin, cocaine, whatever.

'But I *love* my children!' That's just the oxytocin talking. You think you love them because you're a good person, you're responsible, and dutiful, and, well, because they're so loveable, look at them! That's just the oxytocin talking.

All those women (most, according to at least one survey) who didn't really want to become pregnant, but did anyway (because contraception and abortion weren't easily available, and sex was defined as intercourse), and then claimed, smiling, that they wouldn't have it any other way, they love their children – just the oxytocin talking.

The assurance that the labour will be worth it, that you'll forget all about the pain as soon as you see your baby, as soon as you hold your baby – all true. Because of the oxytocin.

Which you'll get more of if you breastfeed.

And which you'll get more of if you have a vaginal birth. Which is why women who intend to give up their babies for adoption or who are surrogates should have caesareans. It'll reduce that drug-induced attachment, making it easier to follow through with their plans. (Why doesn't anyone in tell them that?)

"Roused by the high levels of estrogen during pregnancy, the number of oxytocin receptors in the expecting mother's brain multiplies dramatically near the end of her pregnancy. This makes the new mother highly responsive to the presence of oxytocin." [1] And, "Researchers have found that women's oxytocin levels during their first trimester of pregnancy predict their bonding behavior with their babies during the first month after birth. Additionally, mothers who had higher levels of oxytocin across the pregnancy as well as the postpartum month also reported more behaviors that create a close relationship, such as singing a special song to their baby, bathing and feeding them in a special way, or thinking about them more. Quite simply, the more oxytocin you have, the more loving and attentive you are to your baby." [2]

So those new mothers who *don't* fall in love with their babies? The ones who want to throw them out the window because they're fucking crying all the time? Their brains just didn't produce enough, or perhaps any, oxytocin. Post-partum depression? It's just oxytocin deficiency. (It certainly doesn't mean you're a bad person. I'd throw the kid out the window too.)

And here's the kicker: *oxytocin rewires your brain. Permanently.* "Under the early influence of oxytocin, nerve junctions in certain areas of mother's brain actually undergo reorganization, thereby making her maternal behaviors 'hard-wired.'" [1]

You become a mom. Permanently. Oxytocin makes you sensitive to others' needs (not just your baby's needs, not just your kids' needs). It makes you want to fulfill others' needs. (Not just your baby's needs, not just your kids' needs.) You become nurturing, affectionate, caring. (You become a proper woman? A woman who knows her place?) *Oxytocin changes your personality. It changes you. As any drug does.*

The rest of us, those of us who live oxytocin-free? We don't give a damn. We're not into nurturing others – children *or men*. When we say we don't like kids? We mean it. And when you say 'Oh, just wait until you have some of your own, you'll change your mind!' – you're right. Because we'll become doped up with oxytocin.

So if you don't want to turn into a Mom, if you don't want to dedicate your life to others, to meeting their needs and desires, *Just Say No.*

---

1. http://www.attachmentparenting.org/support/articles/chemistry
2. http://www.ahaparenting.com/ages-stages/pregnancy/oxytocin-pregnancy-birth-mother
3. http://www.psychologicalscience.org/media/releases/2007/feldman.cfm

Ugly, Fat, Hairy Feminists

The reason most feminists are ugly, fat, and hairy is that most feminists are old. That is, over forty.

And there are two good reasons for this. The first is that most living feminists became feminists in the 70s when it was 'in the air' and, therefore, easier to see that women are subordinated in our society. That means they were at least in their late teens in the 70s, which means they're around fifty or sixty now.

The second reason is that too often *it takes until you're forty to figure it out*. Women in their late teens, their twenties, and thirties seem to have it good. They get married. Let's say that means love, a house, and a pension plan. At forty, you get traded in for a younger model. Good-bye to all that.

They have kids. Let's say that means happiness and fulfillment. At forty, they're treated with contempt by their teenagers, dismissed as naïve and incompetent. So much for happiness and fulfillment.

They get interviews; they get jobs. At forty, rather suddenly, it hits you: you're still in the same job, whereas so many of the men around you, even the younger men, have been promoted past you.

So all of this is to say that in your late teens, your twenties, and your thirties, you (seem to) get taken seriously. Sexism? The patriarchy? What are you talking about? But at forty, you stop being taken seriously. You become invisible. No matter what you do. No one hears you. No matter what you say.

And, worse, you suddenly realize that *the only reason* you were *ever* taken seriously was that you were fuckable. Any attention paid to you was pretense. In service to the possibility. You realize that you've been sexualized. Your whole life. Whatever you were had *fem*ale affixed to it. *Pre*fixed to it. You suddenly see the sexism you've been swimming in your whole life.

And, so, you realize you've been subordinated your whole life. Because *female* means *lesser*.

And so you become a feminist.

Of course, there's nothing about being over forty that makes you suddenly ugly, hairy, and fat. (*So-called* ugly, hairy, and fat.) It's being a feminist that makes you so. It's being a feminist that makes you realize that it's against your best interests to accept societal standards about physical appearance – to cover your face with chemical-laden make-up, to inject Botox and silicone; to volumize and style and colour *this* hair, while simultaneously shaving and waxing and plucking *that* hair; to eat less than you need. Because those standards are set *to attract the male gaze*. Those standards keep us sexualized. (In fact, those standards *are* sexualized: beautiful *means* fuckable – which is in large part means young.)

And, so, subordinated.

Plus, quite simply, we have better things to do with our time.

The Trouble with Trans

To the extent that a transperson is someone who experiences body dysphoria, someone who feels they're in the 'wrong' body, someone who feels their body is the 'wrong' sex – how do they know? What is it like to *feel female* (or male)? I was *born* female, and even *I* don't know. So how can *they* know? It's Nagel's 'What is it like to be a bat?' problem. [1] I know what it is to feel healthy only because I have also been sick. I don't know what it is to feel female because I haven't been male. Anything that I feel that I can know *for sure* is due to being female, rather than due to simply being human, is related to having certain, specific body parts – such as a uterus, which can ache and hurt during menstruation, and breasts, which can feel heavy. But there is no 'right' or 'wrong' attached to these feelings.

Other things that I may feel are also certainly due to my body – to its levels of estrogen and progesterone, for example. But they could be due *also* to my body's levels of dopamine and vasopressin, for example. Given the overlapping range of levels of these biochemicals in males and females (many of which are *not* differentiated for males and females), again, how can one say 'I feel this – *because I'm female*'?

Furthermore, feeling like you're in the wrong body implies that there's 'you' and there's 'your body' – which is fine (despite the whole mind/body problem [2]), but, again, if you've never experienced any other body, how can you possible know the one you're in is 'wrong'? And the one of the other sex is 'right'?

I'm not saying body dysphoria isn't real. In fact, I experience every day the mismatch between what's inside and what's outside: I look like a middle-aged woman, but I don't feel like a middle-aged woman. Then again, I do. I must. This must be what a middle-aged woman can feel like. When I say I *don't* feel like a middle-aged woman, I'm using my personal and thus limited experience (my interaction with other middle-aged women) and I'm using stereotypes, pushed at me primarily by profit-seeking marketing departments. Similarly, if you're in a male body, what you feel *must* be male. Maybe it's not the male you see on billboards and television, but it is male nevertheless. (Welcome to our world. [3])

But even so, in this case, I *can* know that my interior doesn't match my exterior: at forty, for example, I know what I felt like at twenty, so when I say I still feel twenty, I know what I'm talking about. I could mean, for example, that my skin feels the same, even though when I look in the mirror, I see that it's lost some of its elasticity. Usually, though, I mean something like I still feel energetic and impassioned, not bland and resigned. But this takes us back to my point about referencing limited experience and stereotypes.

What we need are thorough and carefully conducted studies of MtFs and FtMs. Only an MtF, for example, knows what it felt like when they were flooded with testosterone and what it now feels like to be flooded with estrogen. Sadly, those studies aren't being done, as far as I can tell (which may mean they're just not being publicized). And even if they were, their reliability would be compromised by the nature of subjective report and a (probably) self-selected sample, both of which are likely to be further confounded by the subject's conflation of sex and gender.

Moving onwards. And a little backwards. It seems to me that many transpeople are *actually* saying that their gender doesn't match their sex. That's the disjunct between the 'them' and 'their body'. But if gender is socially constructed, then it's not dependent on sex – so one need not change one's sex in order to change one's gender. In fact, transgendered (as opposed to transsexual) people don't even need their own label. Every woman who refuses to wear make-up and shave her legs is as much a transgendered person as the man who insists on wearing make-up and shaving his legs. [4]

And if it *isn't* socially constructed – that is, if *is* dependent on sex – how do we explain effeminate men and 'tomboys'? How is it that many males use their voice and their hands in a very expressive fashion? How is it that many females are strong and aggressive?

Moving onwards. And again a little backwards. To the label issue. Are MTFs *female*? That depends on how much of how many (and which) primary and secondary sexual characteristics is required to be a member of that sex category. Is a female who has undergone a hysterectomy and a bilateral mastectomy still female? Is a post-menopausal and thus low-estrogen female still female? I'd argue that sex depends on chromosomes: XY is male; XX is female; variations are intersex.

Whether MTFs are *women* is a little trickier because we seem to use the words 'man' and 'woman' to refer to *both* gender and sex. In any case, again, we need a definition: how much, how many, which ...

Of course it *is* possible, by observation and comparison, to identify what it's like to be *treated as* a female/woman. I was born female, raised as a girl, and all of my adult life, treated, by most people most of the time, as a woman. And what does *that* feel like? It feels like shit. To be patronized, marginalized, objectified ... So perhaps a more useful question is '*Should* MTFs be *treated as* women?' Should we pay them less for work of equal value? Should we mock or at least ignore their contributions to society? If we want consistency, yes. If we want justice, no.

On that note, it needs to be said (apparently) that how you're treated affects the person you become. Kick a dog often enough, and it becomes a cowering, fearful mess. The same is true for humans: ignore a person often enough, and she stops speaking up; make her feel like all of her value is in her body, and she obsesses over it; and so on (and so on, and so on). There is a difference between being a FaaB (female assigned at birth) and being an MtF: *a lifetime lived in a female body*. That difference is not inconsequential. To understate. And if MtFs had any understanding at all of sexism, they'd know this. (But perhaps they've been too busy dealing with their dysphoria.) (Or they've just been, well, men.)

So answering the question of whether MtFs are women/females is a no-brainer for the people who've been women/females all their lives. MtFs make demands, not polite requests. [5] They are quick to resort to insult, threat, aggression. They compete. They dominate. They convey a sense of entitlement none of us has ever had. They don't take 'no' for an answer. They scream "WHO THE FUCK ARE YOU TO KEEP US OUT WE HAVE A FUCKING RIGHT TO BE HERE TO GO WHEREVER THE FUCK WE WANT!" – a response to exclusion from FaaB spaces that is "right up there, ideologically, with demanding that girls and women be sexually available visually and physically, for and with men," as Julian Real [6] astutely observes. [7] [8] In short, it quacks like a duck.

In any case, perhaps the most important question is '*Why does it matter?*' – whether one is male or female, a man or a woman. It matters only to those who want to maintain a rigid sex/gender dichotomy. And why would someone want to do that? To support a sexist system/society.

So, I say to MtFs, who are apparently among those who want to maintain such a system/society, if you want to be considered a woman, act like one. Sit down and shut up. Understand that your opinion doesn't count. Be sensitive to everyone else's feelings, respect them, accommodate them. Don't assume you know more than anyone else. In particular, don't assume you know more about sex and gender than second-generation feminists and radfems; they are Ph.D.s (in fact, many of them *have* Ph.D.s) when it comes to sex and gender, and no man *of any kind* comes close to their level of understanding: "[MtFs] lost many of [their] privileges when they started identifying as women," says one such Ph.D., "but rather than recognising that this is because of sexism, they decided it was because they are trans. Why? Because, being male, they knew fuck all about sexism" [9].

It is no surprise to me that twice as many MtFs as FtMs commit suicide. I haven't read many accounts of their transition, but in most of those I have read, I see a shocking naiveté with regard to sexism, gender politics, etc. It's as if these people had no idea that they were voluntarily becoming a member of the sexed subordinate class. So no wonder, on top of everything else, they can't handle, are broadsided by, the sudden and almost complete disenfranchisement …

(So as for the dysphoria – like the person who rejects their leg because it doesn't feel right, because it doesn't feel like it's theirs, isn't it better to deal with the dysphoria than to go through life as an amputee?) (Because yes, being a woman in the patriarchy is, in many ways, like being an amputee. We are crippled. We are, relative to men, dis-abled.)

---

1. http://faculty.arts.ubc.ca/maydede/mind/Nagel_Whatisitliketobeabat.pdf
2. Even if sex is brain-based, and they feel like they have a female brain in a male body – it's the brain that produces hormones. So if they *do* have a female brain, it would be producing estrogen, and there would be no need for hormone treatments.
3. I don't think I've *ever* felt like the women in 99% of the ads and TV.
4. That's assuming that not wearing make-up is not just not-feminine, but is masculine. If it's just not-feminine, then perhaps it's more accurate to call such a woman non-gendered. So would a woman who wears pants instead of a dress be transgendered? Still no. It turns out that aspects of appearance commonly associated with men are more acceptable for women than vice versa. Perhaps that's why there are more men than women seeking to cross the gender divide. Women already can, at least on

superficial matters.
5. At least, those we hear from.
6. http://radicalprofeminist.blogspot.ca/2011/02/who-gets-to-define-women-only-space.html
7. Though one wonders if they're screaming so loudly because they're men or because they're like frogs who have just jumped into a pot of boiling water. (The rest of us women have had a lifetime of to get used to it.) (Poor MTFs, they thought they were going to be special little princesses on a pedestal. What a shock real life must have been.)
8. And so once again, women [FAABs] either stay and fight or thus bullied, silenced, and far too tired, sigh and leave.
9. thebeardedlady, Nov17/09 at https://factcheckme.wordpress.com/2009/11/16/the-fallacy-of-cis-privilege/

The "M" Word on Prime Time TV!!

I'm delightfully surprised by the current season (last) of *Scandal*. I had trouble getting into the show, and actually, I'm surprised I'm still with it; catching a glimpse of a political debate between two women and Melly's bid for the presidency kept me involved, even though I don't really like her, or Olivia ...

And this season, Olivia's arrogance is *really* off-putting, but my god, her 'monument or asterisk' speech to Melly – she actually used the word 'misogyny'. The word! Spoken by a character on prime time TV!! Been waiting for that for almost fifty years.

And then in a subsequent episode, Marcus takes Fitz to task for his white privilege.

And for turning Olivia into a 'black ho'? Bring it on.

And that was *after* he lands that "Welcome to the plight of almost every successful woman in the history of mankind" remark.

Who *are* these writers? And why weren't they on the show since the beginning? (If I'm reading the IMDB site correctly, the writer has always been Shonda Rhimes. Hm.) (Perhaps no surprise: if she'd said the 'm' word in the first episode, perhaps she wouldn't've gotten any further.)

(Though I have to say ... I worry that Olivia will set feminism *back* fifty years if she continues with, well, murder and blackmail. People will say shit like 'See what happens when we let women in power?' conveniently forgetting every man in power that has done the same ...)

Artificial Intelligence Indeed

So I first heard of the movie *Ex Machina* when I read a review (by Chris DiCarlo) in *Humanist Perspectives* – and was so disgusted that I wrote a letter to the editor. Why? Because the reviewer had revealed his own misogyny by failing to address the obvious. The fact that the body the guy created for his AI was that of a female, a sexy female, a young female, is what – mere coincidence? The picture they'd chosen to accompany the review (no doubt, the one chosen to promote the movie) showed her bound. In fishnet.[1] Her pose was right out of a BDSM scene. *Not worth mention?* As I said in my letter,

That you failed to remark on any of this disturbingly telling. It indicates just how much men have come to *expect* to see women as young and sexy. Apparently it's the norm, *it's normal,* to pornify women, to present their bodies as sexually available. Well, fuck you. (Have you heard of sexism? Feminism? Check it out, why don't you.)

The letter was not published. The editor wrote back and said,

I don't know if this changes anything, but Chris had nothing to do with the selection of photos for the review. That was done by a woman who helps me with the onerous task of laying out the magazine.

Which is a comment that opens up a whole 'nother area worth investigation. How is it that people think that if a woman does X, it must be okay (that is, not sexist)? This notion informs the currently popular misconception of feminism as indiscriminate female solidarity. (As a commenter said recently in response to one of my posts on [BlogHer](), implying that I was not a feminist, "My feminist sisters support all woman in whatever choices they make ... " At the very least, that stance would be rife with internal contradictions.)

But onwards. Does it change anything? No. As long as the image is from the movie, then the movie is evidence of the normalized pornification of women, and DiCarlo still ignores that.

If the AI had been black-skinned and called 'boy' and given menial tasks and whipped, I suspect it would have been noticed. I suspect DiCarlo would have made at least passing mention to the implied racism.

But not only is "Ava" a sexy woman-child (there's even a 'play dress up' scene in the movie), the guy has a hall full of closets containing similar AIs. He's not making AIs. He's making fucktoys. He actually tells his (male) guest that they have fully functioning holes. We see him using said holes for his apparent pleasure. The guest realizes that the guy has created Ava to match his (the guest's) porn file. (What the hell is a porn file? Oh.) All very unremarkable, apparently.

There was one promising line (in the movie, not DiCarlo's review): the guy insists that consciousness is gendered. But the claim isn't really challenged. And it becomes clear that he has come to that conclusion because his 'source material' (his 'blue book') for Ava comes from a net cast wide upon the world-as-is. That is, he's just grabbed all the sexist sociocultural conditioning in the world and built something from it. No wonder, Ava.

In short (and this is *my* reveiw), *Ex Machina* is just another movie that objectifies women. It just pretends to be about AI, but it's not even a little bit past Asimov's *I, Robot*.

Is it redeemed by the fact that Ava escapes, after killing the guy (and leaving the guest imprisoned, facing the same outcome)? Not really. Because she does so by sexual manipulation ("I want to be with you," she tells the guest in her soft, little-girl voice. "Do you want to be with me?") [2]. Which is apparently what the script writer and director believe intelligence is – when female-bodied.

And she escapes into the forest wearing high heels – fuck-me heels. Though, okay, that's probably all that was available to her, and we do see that she takes them off. But she doesn't throw them away. Once in the real world, does she choose instead Doc Martens, loose pants with pockets, a comfortable sweatshirt, and a jacket? No. She remains sexualized. *Artificial* intelligence indeed. [3]

---

1. Right, okay, it was actually metal mesh, I get that. And the similarity to fishnet is *also* mere coincidence? (If you think so, you are too naïve for words. Certainly too naïve to be writing movie reviews.)
2. "Yes," I imagine the guest replying. "I'd like the girlfriend experience, please."
3. You know we're laughing at you, right? (When we're not screaming at you.) You who investigate artificial *intelligence* but are too stupid to recognize your own immaturity, you who have conferences on "The Future of Humanity" with all-male panels, you who publish special issues called "Speaking of Humanism" featuring nothing but male faces …

"The Adult Market"

What's adult about coercing someone to do something she doesn't really want to do?
What's adult about humiliating another person?
What's adult about hurting another person?
What's adult about doing sexual things to children?
We should call it what it is. The psychopathic sociopathic misogynist market.

Women Discover Life on Mars

"Should we fund a mission to Mars? Sure. Give us a bit of time and we can make that planet uninhabitable too." (jassrichards.com)

That said, I *thoroughly* enjoyed watching <u>MARS</u>. Why? Because the three astronauts who walk out onto the planet's surface at the end to discover life on Mars are *all women*. Not a token one of three. Not even a remarkable two of three. But ALL THREE. All three are women.

And the bureaucrat back on Earth who makes the announcement? Again, a woman.

And of this was presented as in-your-face feminist. Not one line in the entire script made reference to their *being* women. There was no male resentment, no resistance, no snide comment about quotas or reverse discrimination. There was no undue praise, no celebration for having achieved the status of being the first humans to discover life on Mars.

They just were.

I can't tell you how gratifying it would be to *just be*. To be an astronaut if I wanted to be. To be the one to discover life on Mars. To be the head of a Mars mission program. Just because I was qualified to do so and lucky enough to make it through the selection process. And my sex had as little to do with it as my ear shape.

Furthermore, throughout the expedition, there was as much female presence as male. Sure, okay, one of the women became leader only because one of the men died, but when the second crew arrived, its leader was a woman. And if I'm mistaken about this, it's only because regardless of the actual hierarchy, women were as central, as important, as valuable, as active.

They were just living their lives.

And yet, seven of the eight writers are men. The director is a man. All ten executive producers are men. Even so, they had *three women* discover life on Mars. Three women, all by themselves. They didn't need a man to go with them to protect them. They didn't need a man to go with them in case they got lost.

Amazing. Truly amazing.

And so truly … gratifying. To see this. To actually *see* this. Thank you.

We Won!

"We won!" a neighbor crows to me. Apparently she'd watched a game of some kind on television the night before.

"What 'we'?" I snort. Okay, scoff. "*You* had nothing to do with it." She probably spent the whole game, and much of her life, eating potato chips and drinking beer.

The conversation ends. She can't think about it.

She can't see that her enthusiasm is manufactured. That her 'support' for her team isn't support at all. That 'her' team isn't her team at all. She can't see that she's been deluded into thinking that she's somehow part of it, and that she somehow has a stake in it.

Another neighbor, who'd been watching the Olympics, says the same thing. "We won!"

I point out to her as well that she had nothing to do with it.

"Well," she makes a lame attempt to justify her feelings, "we're Canadian." Right. It was the Canadian team that won.

"I'm Canadian. But when I get a book published, you don't cheer 'We got published!'"

And if you did, I'd smack you upside the head.

How can she feel even a little bit of pride and achievement for the team's victory? She did nothing! Not one push-up, not one lap around the track.

"Well," she tries again, "I support the team with my taxes."

"And you support my writing with your taxes as well. Whenever I get a grant from the Arts Council," I explain.

She still doesn't see it. (Or simply *won't* see it.) She doesn't see that her emotions are being manipulated by the sports corporations, who want to deliver as many potential customers as possible to the companies who buy the advertisements that pay their salaries, because the more viewers, the more they can charge for those advertisements. [1]

---

1. Quite apart from that, it's no coincidence that sports are dominated by men. (Which makes *her* 'We won!' just a little bit ironic.) Or, rather, it's no coincidence that it's predominantly men's sports that get television coverage. It's just another way of making sure men are the center of the universe. My god, how many television stations are devoted to *just* sports? Why in god's name does sport get a regular time slot in the daily news? As if men playing a game is as important as a war! And *more* important than the destruction of our environment (which *doesn't* get a regular time slot in the daily news)!

Congratulations

'Congratulations!' Now there's a word we misuse a lot.

'I'm getting married!' 'Congratulations!' Why? Why should this be cause for congratulations? Is it a good thing? Half of all married couples end up divorced. (The other half just couldn't be bothered.) Is it an achievement? There are no qualifications except being a certain age. Which generally happens without any effort. So you're entering into a legal contract with another person. Big deal. Bet you haven't even read the contract. So you're going to a church for some obscure sacrament. What, Christmas and Easter wasn't enough?

What's getting married really about? Proof you're not gay after all. Proof that you're all grown up, gonna settle down, maybe start a family (like having a kid means *you're* no longer a kid is the logic, I guess). Proof that someone somewhere somehow found you loveable long enough to agree to marriage. Yeah right, whatever.

'I'm pregnant!' 'Congratulations!' What? Again, is this necessarily a good thing? 'Cause it can seldom be called an achievement. I mean I'm sure you have succeeded at sexual intercourse before. So you got lucky. Should we congratulate for luck?

'I won the lottery!' ' Congratulations!' It sounds right. But it sure takes the wind out of the congratulations we give to the person who wins a triathlon or a Beethoven competition.

Getting Married

When you 'get married' you are entering into a legal contract. You might be doing a few other things (promising your love to someone, making a deal with a god), but you are most certainly entering into a legally binding contract with another person. There are rights due to and responsibilities incumbent upon people who enter into a marriage contract. Some of these have to do with money, some have to do with children, some have to do with sexual services, and some have to do with other things.

What I find so extremely odd is that even though well over 90% of all people in the USA and Canada get married, almost none of them read the terms of the contract before they sign. (Most people find out about these terms only when they want to break the contract.) Probably because the contract isn't presented when their signatures are required.

Although this begs the question 'Is the contract, therefore, still binding?', the more interesting question is '*Why* isn't it presented?'

Reading/Watching the News: A Bad Habit

Why do you read the paper (or watch the news) every day? Certainly not for an objective account of what's going on in the world. Because surely you're aware of editorial bias: what gets in (or not), where it goes, and how much space it gets there. And reporter bias: who gets interviewed, what gets asked (or not), what gets put at the beginning of the piece, and how it's said.

To describe an incident with complete objectivity is to give a phenomenological account. And anyone who's taken Phenomenology 101 knows how difficult that is. Even to say "There is a brown house" is to have made an assumption, is to have imposed your subjectivity. You can't see the house. From your perspective, standing in front of it, all you see is one, or maybe two walls. You *assume* there's a third and a fourth. Your subjectivity fills in the gaps. *All the time.*

It gets worse. Is the glass half empty or half full? One description is positive, the other is negative.

And worse still. Consider something as simple as an accident report. You begin with "A serious accident occurred ... " Well, right away you're in trouble. Who says it's serious? How serious *is* serious? Serious to who? You've expressed your opinion. Furthermore, you've assumed it was an *accident*. My guess it that you didn't speak to the drivers. Maybe it was intentional.

Try again. To say "A *ran into* B" is to put it in rather aggressive terms. "A *hit* B" is almost as bad. "*Car* A hit *Car* B" is a little better. "Car A *collided with* Car B" is even better, but still you've suggested that A is to blame (because it did the doing – colliding or whatever); maybe Car B *got in the way of* Car A. "Car A and Car B collided" is better still, but only "Car A and Car B occupied the same space at the same point in time" is

229

really objective.

Now consider the difficulty of reporting something involving more than inanimate objects. For example, people. Consider "The fight continues between the Board and the Union ... " To call it a *fight* is to describe a whole set of attributes (animosity, competition) which may or may not be present. And, in any case, I don't think everyone agrees on when an interaction involving those attributes actually becomes a *fight* – again, it's a subjective call. "The struggle to find a common ground continues ... " is better, but still, you've called it a struggle, you've again put your own opinion into the report. To say "The negotiations continued ... " is perhaps most accurate, most objective. But you'd better stop there: even to add "for yet another day" suggests it's going on too long – an opinion. The thing is this: purely objective reports are boring; to make the news interesting, to sucker you into reading it, it's made subjective.

It's also made exciting. Loud noises are exciting. At the very least, they get our attention. And conflict, more than resolution, seems associated with loud noises. So conflict gets covered more than resolution. And things involving neither get covered *as if* they were conflicts, as if there is some problem, some difficulty. (And certainly any problem or difficulty that *is* there gets emphasized, even exaggerated.) So you read the paper for excitement (get a life) – but not only is it *vicarious* excitement, it's *fabricated*, *fake* excitement.

Even if the news accounts *were* objective, why do you read so many of them every day? (Now *commentary*, that would actually be useful – it could make sense of the accounts.) I just want to know what's going on, people say. But why? Does it give you a feeling of control to know? Anyone who gave it half a thought would feel less, not more, powerful knowing about problems they could not or would not solve.

Perhaps you mistake passive participation for active

participation. Reading about something exciting or important makes you feel exciting or important.

Truth is, people read the paper because, well, people have always read the paper – it's what you do, every morning at the breakfast table or every day after work with a drink. People in general are a rather thoughtless bunch. And they pay with the skewered world view they thereby acquire.

Vote? WTF?

So I noticed the "Question of the Day" feature on the Weather Network website, which typically poses a question along with four response options, inviting site visitors to "Vote". I haven't done a survey, but I suspect this sort of thing is not unusual.

Which makes it all the more disturbing.

Why? Because often the question is a matter of fact. For example, on September 5, the question was "Which of these animals is Saskatchewan's provincial animal?" And four options were provided: Caribou, White-tailed deer, Bison, Spirit bear, Big horn sheep. [1]

To vote means to express your preference as part of a *decision-making* process. Voting *on facts* is an oxymoron. (What, if the majority believe the world is flat, it is?) The feature should be titled "Test your knowledge" and invite site visitors to indicate the correct answer.

It would be disturbing enough if it was just an incorrect use of our language. Or, if not evidence of ignorance, then evidence of sloppiness, of inattentiveness. Because this is not some obscure little site. This is The Weather Network.

And along with such relentless requests for feedback at every second site and the ubiquitous 'Like' feature, the effect of such 'voting' is to make us feel engaged with the world when we are so not. It instils a false sense of self-worth in people who are, let's be frank, pretty worthless. [2]

---

1. Other times, the question is something like "Did this summer feel longer, shorter, or the same as other summers?" And site visitors are invited to "view the results". What self-respecting adult *cares* or is even *curious* about such a thing?

2. Only in part because they're taking the time to express their opinions on such trivial matters. And probably *not* taking the time to develop and express informed opinions on

matters of importance.

Speaking in Code

"I just can't give any more, sorry." But of course he can. He just doesn't want to. By saying "can't" instead of "won't", however, he appears powerless and thus absolves himself of responsibility; as a result, we don't even consider the matter of blame.

"That's not gonna happen." Okay. So informed, we move on. But in most cases, the accurate, honest, statement would have been "*I don't think* that's gonna happen" or "*I don't want* that to happen." By presenting an opinion as fact, the speaker has diverted our attention from evidence and reasons. *Why* don't you think that's going to happen? *Why* don't you want that to happen?

"We need to bring our product in line with contemporary standards." The royal "we" effects a diffusion of responsibility, deflecting accountability from the individual who's speaking. "Need" is a lie: we won't die without it. But "need" is far more *compelling* than "want" – it's harder to refuse. To "bring in line" suggests cooperation, rather than obedience. "Contemporary" sounds so much better than "common" or even "current", and "standards" implies something that's received official, i.e., expert, approval. Really, he's just saying "I want you to do what I want: this." And *that* would be much easier to say "No" to.

"Hey now, what kind of way is that to talk?" Code for "I don't want to hear those words" – to which the person might simply respond, "So?" Instead, he or she feels chastised.

These manipulations are done so smoothly, it's impressive. I have enough trouble getting clear about my true meaning, I couldn't possibly engage in the simultaneous translation these people seem to do so effortlessly in order to cover their truth and manipulate us into assent, or at least out of dissent. They load their language without even thinking. How can they be so quick, so clever?

They're not. They *are* doing it without even thinking. They're not translating from A to B – they're going right to B; they're not even aware of A. I've been attributing far more consciousness than is warranted. It's not that they're thinking more (let alone more quickly) than me – they're thinking less: they're not thinking at all about what they're saying, about how they're saying it. Consider that when I point out what I think they *really* mean, when I decode what they say in order to challenge or simply clarify, they insist I'm reading too much into a simple choice of words – I'm over-analyzing. Truth is, they're not analyzing enough. Or at all.

But still, how is it they are so unconsciously manipulative? It just comes naturally. And that's far scarier than doing it intentionally. All those manipulative phrases – these people are simply saying it the way they've been conditioned to say it, or, more accidentally, just the way they've heard others say it.

So it's not that I'm a relative moron at strategic behaviour; it's that somehow I missed out on that conditioning. Probably because I'm not male. And I consciously rejected any parallel conditioning directed to females.

So here I am. Either taking what people say at face value and being manipulated left, right, and centre, or trying to decode everything. Of course, by the time I decode what they've said, B into A, they've said something else. And when I respond directly to A, they think I've gone off-topic. So I have to explain that their B is a translation of A. But they don't want to hear it. I suppose I could just respond to their B with a B of my own – but to do that, I have to decode their B into A, figure out my response to it, then encode my A into a B. And by the time I've done that, they've left. Which is just as well.

If you can't say anything nice, don't say anything at all.

What? Why is honesty rude? What kind of society considers honesty, *truth*, to be less important than – what? Social cohesion?

Furthermore, that assumes that people will be offended by the truth. If the truth is about them, I suppose that's an accurate assumption. But what does *that* say? About people.

And actually, even if the truth *isn't* about them, I suspect many people would be offended by the truth *when it challenges their own views*. And what does *that* say?

More likely, truth has simply been trumped by self-interest. Because if honesty *does* offend, for whatever reason, then the truth-speaker will be alienated, ostracized – a social outcast. (Though, as far as I'm concerned, social inclusion is of dubious value ...)

But if we'd've been honest every time rights collide, speaking up about the limits of freedoms, perhaps everyone wouldn't feel so frickin' entitled all the time. To everything.

And if we'd've called each other out, on anything, on everything, we'd be leading more authentic lives.

Many of my neighbours have their TVs on all the time; as a result, they do very little thinking on their own. Not only because there is no silence, typically required for thought, but also because they're exposing themselves so relentlessly to a worldview censored by a handful of conglomerates motivated primarily by self-interest. And then, *because* there's nothing going on in their heads, they can't stand the silence, so they keep the TV on all the time ... But do I say 'Shut that thing off and wake the fuck up!'? Of course not. That would be rude.

A couple of them also take RV trips. Do I point out that

they're leaving a *huge* ecological footprint, that they've contributed to climate change, that they're partly responsible for the increasing number and severity of storms, and that, therefore, they've been rather selfish and inconsiderate? No. I ask whether they had a good trip. Pleasant superficiality has become a habit.

When I see a woman performing femininity, do I tell her she's making it hard for those of us who'd like to be taken seriously, for our knowledge and our skills, not for our clownface and fuck-me-heels? No.

Those of us with half a brain, who are trying to live a true and morally responsible life – we've been polite too long. We've been silent too long. We've been *dishonest* too long.

In Praise of Dead Air

People are uncomfortable with silence. On the radio, over the telephone, in person. It's a curious thing.

We are obsessed with filling up the air space. That sounds very male – the need to occupy territory (take a look at how men sit, their legs wide apart and their arms resting on the backs of the adjacent chairs, compared to how women sit, legs close together and their hands in their laps) – but women too consider dead air problematic.

Is it that we're afraid to say 'I'll have to think about that'? Because thinking about it is for philosophers, contemplatives, monks? Ordinary people who think are so odd, they're commented upon – 'a penny for your thoughts'. (And so poor at thinking, their thoughts are worth only a penny?)

Or is it that we're afraid to say 'I don't know'? Men especially seem unable to get those words out. (I assume this is related to their inability to stop and ask for directions.) Better a poor response than no response at all. More often than not, better a lie.

So we don't say these things. We chatter instead. We fill the air with small talk. Is it that noise suggests activity? If you're a child, I guess you think so. But even so, activity is not *necessarily* good. Am I back to the male thing? *They're* the ones obsessed with *action*: they start with action figures, then go on to action movies, and big team action sports, and finally it all gets sublimated into the task-oriented Type A personality. But it's women too. Rule #4 of 'How to be a Good Date' is all about the art of conversation, i.e. *how to keep it going*. Dead air is embarrassing. Dead air is rude.

I suggest not. I suggest that the *absence* of dead air is what's rude. Nonstop patter allows no time to think; in fact, it discourages thought. So when you aim for a conversation, what you get is very superficial. You can't ask good questions if you're trying to get instant responses. And if, by mistake, a good question *is* asked, you can't take time to consider it if you're afraid of dead air – so you *don't* really consider it. And isn't *that* rude? Not taking the other person's comments and questions seriously?

Perhaps those who call it dead air are themselves dead – unable, or worse, unwilling, to think. Dead air can be alive, bustling with the work of understanding what was just said, and then of judging it – right? wrong? important? trivial? Can I add to it? change it? use it? Only those unaccustomed to mental activity would mistake silence for *in*activity.

YouTube: 300 hours per minute [1]

300 hours are uploaded to YouTube per minute. *300 hours* every *minute*! How is it that so many people think so much of their stuff warrants public attention?

On the one hand, I love the absence of corporate and editorial control at the gate: the former motivated almost exclusively by personal financial interest (i.e., selfish greed), the latter only somewhat less so (it has the dubious advantage of being motivated also by someone's definition of artistic value, at least in the case of artistic performance), both bound to be unfair to many individuals and detrimental to society as a whole.

But geez louise, people, use a little self-censorship! *Not everything you do deserves everyone's attention!* Have you no standards? Or just no respect for others? (I really lose it when I see videos of performances *known* to be flawed – "This is just my first try" or "I know I made a few mistakes, but … " Then redo it! Do it again and again until you get it right! Practice! Revise! Spend the time it takes, make the effort required, to achieve excellence.) (In the meantime, shame on you for wasting my attention, wasting my time, with your mediocrity.)

But then, "*everyone's* attention" – maybe most people who post to YouTube are really doing it just to show family and friends. But then why don't they post on their limited access Facebook page?

And, too, "*deserves*" – is that an anachronistic view? Appropriate only when resources are limited, and so justifiably reserved for the best? No, I don't think so. Because even when space is unlimited – perhaps *especially* when space is unlimited – if a pearl is buried in a pile of shit, who's going to spend time looking for it? The bigger the pile, the more difficult, and eventually we'll stop looking. Which defeats the purpose.

(Doesn't it? What *is* YouTube's purpose?)

---

1. When I first wrote this piece, it was 13 hours per minute.

Digital Thought

On/off, yes/no, either/or, for/against, male/female, win/lose, true/false, right/wrong, black/white, all/nothing. 0/1.

Why have we become so enamoured with digital thought? What's the attraction?

It's precise. Precision is good.

It's fast. We like that.

It's easy. We like that even more.

But any educator will tell you that T/F tests are the sparrows of measurement. They can handle knowledge, and maybe comprehension. [1] But that's it.

And yet, because it's the only thought that computers, including the ubiquitous automated answering systems, are capable of, digital thought is becoming even *more* dominant. [2]

But knowledge and comprehension are the lowest levels on Bloom's taxonomy of cognitive skills. What about application? Analysis? Synthesis? Evaluation? What, no time for *critical* thought? Too busy surfing the net to notice you're in an ocean of shit?

Most of life isn't subject to precision, isn't true or false, black or white. One of the many errors in reasoning is the false dichotomy: it occurs when one assumes, *erroneously*, that there are only two possibilities. So digital thought leaves out a lot. It's woefully incomplete.

And it encourages extremism. Because it ignores the richness of a continuum, a spectrum. Between all and nothing is something. Lots of somethings.

And it fosters competition. It has no room for compromise, for combination.

In short, it's two dimensional. Frogs do it: if it moves, it's food; if it doesn't, don't bother. Are we frogs? Yes/No.

1. Multiple choice tests, the robins, are just one step better. (Except for the LSAT, the smartass bluejay, which is designed by demented geniuses who have made a science of turning a curve ball into a triple helix and figured out how to get paid for doing it.)
2. Did I say 'dominant'? I meant 'domineering'.

Asking the Right Questions

Never has it been more important to ask the right questions. Not as philosophers, in the clearest, most explicit, terms, but in terms most likely to be used by the arrested-development minds of computer programmers. Because phone conversations, for example, aren't with people anymore; they're with AI programs that are, let's face it, stupider than most people. (Which is saying a lot.)

And that's because they're designed by people with no philosophical training [1], by people who think in terms of black and white, people whose imaginations seem to be severely limited. Which means you have to stay within a severely limited range of possibilities in order to be understood; you have to anticipate how such a simple mind might say something.

I imagine a very near future in which the stupid people succeed because they're the only ones able to communicate with all our 'smart' programs [2] – because their minds are unclouded by complexity and subtlety.

---

1. It takes a lot of skill, a lot of knowledge and intelligence, to craft an exhaustive menu of options, and one whose items are mutually exclusive.
2. "Welcome to FedEx! In a few words, please tell me what you're calling about." Took me ten tries.

Good Intentions: The Road to Hell
(and justifiably so)

I've reconsidered intent-based moralities. They're bloody irresponsible. I'm giving new meaning to "The road to hell is paved with good intentions" (or maybe I'm just finally understanding it). Intention-based moralities are for people too stupid or too lazy to consider the consequences of their actions. "But I didn't mean to" is the cry of an idiot. (What did you think would happen when you put a firecracker in the dog's mouth?) "I was only trying to help" is an attempt to absolve oneself of the burden of figuring out the effect one's behavior has on others. (In what universe is *that* helpful?) If you only meant to have a bit of fun, getting in your car drunk out of your mind and driving down the 401, if you didn't intend to hurt anyone, well then, okay, you can go (you *should* go) – to hell.

Planning is Sinister?

In *This Changes Everything*, Naomi Klein makes an interesting observation, intended to explain why we *aren't* building the kind of economy we need: " ... there is something sinister, indeed vaguely communist, about *having a plan* to build the kind of economy we need, even in the face of existential crisis" (125, my emphasis).

Is that why we don't plan?

At the individual level. People are so *que sera* even about creating other human beings. 'You're pregnant? I didn't know you wanted to spend twenty years of your life looking after someone.' 'Oh, it just happened ... .'

And at the community level. If, for example, lakes were zoned according to use – jetskiers and motorboats here, people-with-screaming-kids-who-need-to-be-safe here, and canoeists and kayakers here – everyone could be happy. But as it is, there's a lot of anger going around.

This lack of planning – it's all *because it's communist*? *Because a pre-determined society is somehow* against *individual freedom*? *Not* planning is against individual freedom. Not planning is allowing yourself to be tossed about at random, by chance – and that's not being free.

I wonder if there's also a religious element involved. To plan, to choose your future, is to reject, or at least challenge, God's plan. For you, your future.

Also, planning requires foresight, and foresight requires imagination. Which, I'm realizing, most people don't have.

Planning also requires strong desires, for X over Y. Again, I'm realizing that most people – don't really care. (Which means they get in the way of those of us who do.)

Every Day in Every Way

Every day in every way the world is getting better and better. Yeah right.

Well why isn't it? Every day there's a whole new batch of young adults just chafing at the bit to change the world. What happens?

They become parents.

So first, there's the matter of money. Nutritious food and a constant supply of clothing that fits cost money. Leaving little for the revolution.

Then there's the matter of time. To get the money, you need to work. So that pretty much makes the day a write-off. And much of the evening is taken up with parenting. It's nine o'clock: do you have time to change the world – before you go to bed?

Better question: do you have the energy to change the world? Getting up at six or seven, hustling the kids and yourself to daycare, school, and work, putting in eight hours that is, no doubt, laced with at least a little stress, making your way home, perhaps detouring to pick up a kid or two, making supper for several people, doing the dishes, then slogging through a bunch of chores like washing everyone's clothes, or cleaning the house or apartment a little, or preparing lunches, all the while spending quality time with the kids – it's nine o'clock: do you know where your bed is?

But more significant than any of that is this: parents don't take risks. You can't afford to get fired – so you don't stand up at work. You can't afford to go to jail – so you don't stand up anywhere else. You're responsible for your kids, they depend on you, you have obligations to them – to be there and to provide them with what they need. You can't afford to be reckless anymore; you become cautious – about everything.

Because you love them so much – if anything should ever happen to them – So you don't make enemies; at least, none that really count. Love holds you hostage, it makes you vulnerable; it makes you – oh dear – conservative.

And *that's* why young radicals become middle-aged sell-outs overnight: they have kids.

And parents don't change the world.

(They hope their kids will.)

(But, of course, their kids will grow up and have …

"If my wife will let me."

"If my wife will let me." That's what Richard Branson said when he was asked whether he'd go to Mars: "It may be a one-way trip ... . So maybe I'll wait till the last ten years of my life, and then maybe go, if my wife will let me" (Klein, *This Changes Everything*, p.288). Does he really think no one will notice how inauthentic he was being? He's one of the most powerful men in the world. He doesn't need anyone's permission for anything.

On top of that, he doesn't want to take her with him?

And on top of *that*, she doesn't have a name? (I'm surprised he didn't say 'the wife' rather than 'my wife' – to underscore his view that women are all just so interchangeable.)

It's tiresome. Wife/girlfriend as Mom. So the man can continue to be a child, just one of the boys. Wife/girlfriend as authority. See, I'm not sexist, women have the *real* power.

Even from our most intelligent, most capable, men.

So very tiresome.

Men Need to Reclaim the Moral

Something I noticed when I taught Business Ethics, primarily to male students, is that men seem to think ethics is 'a girl thing'. What? *What?!* (My god, that can explain *everything!*)

Men routinely insult other men who express concern about doing the right thing – "What are you, a fucking boy scout?" Note that boy scouts are children.

Worse, men who raise ethical questions are accused of going *soft*, being *weak*, being a bleeding *heart*. Note that these qualities are associated with being female. It's thus *emasculating* to be concerned about right and wrong. *What?!*

Furthermore, ethics presumes caring, and real men don't care. They may protest that they can't 'afford' to care; they have to make real decisions about profit and war, and feelings just get in the way. As if ethics is all, only, about feelings. (Where did they get their education? Oh, they didn't. We don't actually *teach* ethics. Except in a few university courses.)

The problem with all this is that men run the world. And it's not going well.

So isn't it about time men reclaim the moral? If rising above the gendered worldview is too much, then just redefine your terms a bit – and ... *Man up! Consider* (and then *do*) the right thing!

Oh the horror.

On yet another occasion during which I was stunned by one of my neighbour's stupidity and ignorance, it suddenly occurred to me that the person I was speaking with probably hadn't read a book since high school. [1]

Then it occurred to me that that was probably true for *most* people.

I tried to imagine what that would be like. What my mind would be like if I hadn't read a book, not one book, in the last, say, forty years.

Oh the horror.

Because what could possibly go on inside such a mind?

In addition to their high school history and geography textbooks, through which they might have plodded here and there, they might have read, perhaps, a dozen novels, in all. Library books for the annual book review assignment in English class. Who is the main character? Describe the setting. What is the main conflict?

They may as well be illiterate. They *are*, essentially. They're *functionally* illiterate. Because yes, they can and probably do read package labels and price tags, but *what else?*

The newspaper. Which is pretty much nothing but exposition. Low-level description. No analysis. No critique.

What if everyone read just one non-fiction book a week? What if employers rewarded them for doing so, as many of them do now for physical exercise: in addition to so many points per kilometer, because it reduces their healthcare costs, so many points per page, because – Ah, there's the rub. What's in it for them? Nothing. In fact, on the contrary, it's to their advantage *not* to have their employees develop knowledge, understanding, critical ability.

Okay, so what if the *government* implemented such a reward program? Well, it's not really in their best interests either. Which explains, perhaps, why the education system doesn't mandate critical thinking courses.

Of course, if *parents* ... But every time they say 'Because I said so,' they stomp on critical thinking. It's just easier that way, I guess.

So in whose interests *is* it be critical? Our own, of course. Otherwise, we're suckers to manipulation by media. Corporations. Government. Anyone who puts their own self-interest before yours.

But in our society, the word 'critical' has negative connotations. It's bad to be critical.

Oh the horror.

---

1. Yes, it then occurred to me that s/he probably hadn't read a book *during* high school either.

Calm down. Don't think about – Don't think.

One day when I was talking to a neighbour about something that I wished we could do something about – someone tossing their garbage out of their car onto the road where we walk every day, someone letting their kid drive a dirt bike with no muffler throughout the neighbourhood, someone burning leaves and sending toxic smoke everywhere, can't remember – she said something like 'Calm down, your blood pressure's going up!'

Well, it wasn't (ten years after I stopped running forty miles a week, my blood pressure has finally crept up into the normal range), but I realized then that she wasn't distinguishing between what I was doing – making a point about civility, and respect for others, and the difference between public and private space, and speculating about the possibility of change – and some emotional rant that might end in screaming and slamming doors. I suppose the latter *can* elevate one's blood pressure, and if it's high to begin with, high enough that you're on blood pressure medication (as she is), then yeah – calm down. You're giving yourself a heart attack.

Later, it occurred to me that a lot of people today have high blood pressure, and probably half of the people I'm likely to talk to (my neighbours) are probably on high blood pressure medication, no wonder they, people, develop a sort of blind and deaf veneer. No wonder they just 'go with the flow' and never object. No wonder they avoid thinking about – Well, thinking. It's literally bad for their health. Life-threatening, even.

But what this means – this inability to distinguish argument from rage, along with the increasing number of people with high blood pressure – is that the more we eat at McDonald's, the less we'll get angry about McDonald's. The more zombied out people are, sprawled on the couch in front of the TV, the more zombied out people will strive to remain. Sprawled on the couch in front of the TV.

Not thinking.

www.ingramcontent.com/pod-product-compliance
Lightning Source LLC
Chambersburg PA
CBHW031638040426
42453CB00006B/141